The Way We Really Live:
Social Change in Metropolitan Boston
Since 1920

National Endowment for the Humanities

Learning Library Program

Boston Public Library

Publication No. 4

**The Way We Really Live:
Social Change in Metropolitan Boston
Since 1920**

by
Sam Bass Warner, Jr.
William Edwards Huntington Professor
of History and Social Sciences,
Boston University

Lectures Delivered for the
National Endowment for the Humanities
Boston Public Library
Learning Library Program

Boston, Trustees of the Public Library of
the City of Boston, 1977

Copyright © 1977 by the Trustees of the
Public Library of the City of Boston

Library of Congress Cataloging in Publication Data:

Warner, Sam Bass, Jr., 1928-
  The way we really live.

  "Lectures delivered for the Humanities, Boston Public Library,
Learning Library Program Boston."
    Bibliography: p. 107, 108.
    1. Boston—Social conditions—Addresses, essays, lectures.
  2. Boston—Economic conditions—Addresses, essays, lectures.
  I. Boston. Public Library. National Endowment for the Humanities.
Learning Library Program. II. Title.
HN80.B7W32   309.1'744'6104   77-28418
ISBN 0-89073-053-9

Permissions:

Permission has been granted to quote excerpts from the following:
American Folklore Society—"Many Positions to Be Eliminated," *Urban Folklore From the Paperwork Empire*, by Alan Dundes and Carl R. Pagter.
Harcourt, Brace, Jovanich, Inc.—"The Machine Stops," *The Eternal Moment and Other Stories*, by E. M. Forster.
Houghton, Mifflin, Inc.—*Stella Dallas*, by Olive Higgins Prouty.
G. P. Putnam, Inc./Berkley Publishing Corp.—"Slow Sculpture," *Sturgeon Is Alive and Well*, by Theodore Sturgeon.
Random House, Inc./Alfred A. Knopf, Inc.—*Couples*, by John Updike.
Scribner's, Inc.—*The Great Gatsby*, by F. Scott Fitzgerald.

Cover: LANDSAT Infrared Satellite Photograph, South of Boston, Including Cape Cod
Photograph courtesy of the National Aeronautics amd Space Administration.

Contents

List of Tables   vii
List of Figures   ix
Introduction   xi

I. Slow Growth and Rapid Change   1
II. A Stable Population   17
III. The Family and the Metropolitan Economy   27
IV. A Humane Economy   41
V. The Peaceable Kingdom   51
VI. The Metropolitan Zoo   60
VII. The Symbolic Climate   74
VIII. A Mirror for Strangers   83
Reference Bibliography   107

List of Tables

I-A. Boston BEA: Population and Population Growth, 1920-1970   11

II-A. Composition of Families, 1970   23

III-A. A Scenario for Three Average Boston Families, 1920-1970   28-30

III-B. Distribution of Aggregate Personal Income by Families, United States, 1935/36, 1964   38

IV-A. 1930: Tri-State Area, Persons 10 Years Old and Over Engaged in Gainful Occupations, by Industry   46

IV-B. 1970: Tri-State Area, Experienced Civilian Labor Force 16 Years and Older by Industry   47

List of Figures

I-1. United States Air Force Satellite Photograph of the United States at Night 3
I-2. LANDSAT Infrared Satellite Photograph, North of Boston, Including Cape Ann and Southern New Hampshire 4
I-3. LANDSAT Infrared Satellite Photograph, South of Boston, Including Cape Cod 5
I-4. Population Distribution in the United States, 1970 6
I-5. Suffolk County Commuting Patterns, 1970 7
I-6. Five Inner Boston County Commuting Patterns, 1970 8
I-7. Providence County Commuting Patterns, 1970 9
I-8. Population Shift, 1920-1930 12
I-9. Population Shift, 1930-1940 13
I-10. Population Shift, 1940-1950 14
I-11. Population Shift, 1950-1960 15
I-12. Population Shift, 1960-1970 15
II-1. Population Fifteen Years and Older, Married, Tri-State Area, Percent 22
II-2. Annual Rate of Divorce Per One Hundred Women Fifteen Years and Older, United States, 1920-1972 24
II-3. Women in Broken Families Per One Hundred Married Women Fifteen Years and Older, Tri-State Area, 1920 and 1970 25
III-1. Employment Changes in the New England Textile Industry, 1956-1965 32
III-2. Employment Changes in the New England Shoe and Leather Industry, 1956-1965 32
III-3. Employment Changes in the New England Electrical Machinery Industry, 1956-1965 33
III-4. White Males, Average Yearly Wages, 1973, by Counties as Percentage of White Male Wages in Highest Wage County 33
III-5. Black Males, Average Yearly Wages, 1973, by Counties as Percentage of White Male Wages in Highest Wage County 34
III-6. White Females, Average Yearly Wages, 1973, by Counties as Percentage of White Male Wages in Highest Wage County 35
IV-1. Per Capita Income by Percent of Wealthiest County, 1926 41
IV-2. Per Capita Income by Percent of Wealthiest County, 1970 42
V-1. Edward Hicks, "Peaceable Kingdom" (oil on canvas), 1844 54
VI-1. Annual Estimated Sulfur Dioxide Levels, 1975 64
VI-2. Annual Estimated Total Suspended Particulate Levels, 1975 65
VI-3. Water Resources of the Neponset and Weymouth River Basins 67
VIII-1. "Project Swing" I 85
VIII-2. "Project Swing" II 86
VIII-3. "Screwed" 87
VIII-4. through VIII-35. Mass Magazine Images from the 1920's to the 1970's 92-105

Introduction

The Public Library is one of our favorite institutions here in Boston. It is so popular among us because it encourages us to be what we may be, and to become what we will. Although we may be mean and angry, screaming and fighting with one another in the streets, as we often are in this city, the Boston Public Library stands quietly as a symbol of what our city can do. Even though our city fathers may be locked into one of their perennial shouting matches, they pause long enough to vote a generous appropriation for the Library, and in that pause they honor the pride we all take in this enduring manifestation of the possibilities which lie within the plurality of our community.

On a typical weekday at the main Library in Copley Square one finds kindergarten teachers clogging the check-out lines with their stacks of picture books, young girls deep into the next volume of an adventure series, a film running on the exploration of outer space, nearby apartment dwellers with stacks of records in their arms, old people dozing over their books in the sunny courtyard, young lawyers burrowing through reports in the documents room, types like myself pestering the reference librarians in a vain search for the antecedents of an imperfect footnote, college students grinding at the long tables in the old reading room, the announcement of a small course in the new accounting, and preparations for an evening reception in honor of the hanging of another addition to the print collection. And nowhere can one find a more concentrated gathering of hopes and fantasies than in the small room set aside for newspaper readers. The lecture series, from which this book derives, is but another addition to the seemingly endless variety of the Library.

On the occasion of the Bicentennial of the United States, and in conjunction with the many events taking place in Boston during those two years, the Library, with the assistance of the National Endowment for the Humanities, launched a series of lectures and informal courses on the history of the city. The subjects were presented by specialists and ordered both chronologically and thematically so that one could review the city's political history, study colonial times, or examine its architecture, literature, or labor history. My task was to summarize recent trends in the Boston metropolis since 1920.

The audience for the lectures filled the Library's large auditorium each evening and their enthusiasm spurred us all on to a level of performance we rarely achieve in our classrooms. The challenge for the lecturer lay in the variety of the listeners and the wide range of their training and interests. Unlike the typical classroom, no one was required to attend, and unlike the college classroom persons of every age from high school students to retired businessmen, and every training from grammar school dropouts to college professors were present in the hall. All of us who taught found this challenge to think clearly and to say clearly what we had to say extraordinarily stimulating. Indeed the response to the lectures and informal classes proved once again that the Boston Public Library is a place where expert and layman can meet for a profitable interchange between scholarship and life experience. So successful, indeed, has the experiment been, that the Library and the National Endowment are working to make the Learning Library series a permanent addition to the Copley Square offerings.

In my own case special circumstances made it possible for me to participate in the program. A John Simon Guggenheim Foundation Fellowship and a Humanities Fellowship of the Rockefeller Foundation enabled me to devote myself full time to beginning a research project on the recent history of the Boston metropolis. These lectures are, thus, a kind of progress report, some of my initial discoveries. I hope in time these beginnings will mature into a new kind of urban history.

The study of a metropolis is necessarily more complicated than even the history of one large city, and to make the progress I did required the assistance of many knowledgeable people. Lloyd Rodwin of the Department of Urban Studies and Planning at M.I.T. lent his experience and imagination to the original conception of the lecture series. The Library staff brought its skills to bear on all manner of problems of research and presentation. Especially I want to thank Paul M. Wright, head of the Learning Library Program, and Yen-Tsai Feng, Assistant Director in charge of the Research Library, in this connection. Diana J. Kleiner has assisted me at every step in finding a path through a jungle of references and has been patient with many a half-baked research lead, and the dogged bibliographic efforts of Julie Ming Tai have saved me many hours.

My research into the demographic attributes of the metropolis was aided by the suggestions of Alvin J. Sanders of the Massachusetts Office of State Planning and Management, and by data provided me by Jerome Clubb and Erik Austin of the Inter-University Consortium for Political and Social Research at the University of Michigan.

Henry L. DeGraff of the United States Department of Commerce, Bureau of Economic Analysis, furnished essential employment data, as did Alexander Ganz, Director of Research of the Boston Redevelopment Authority. My friend Jeffrey May helped me with crucial economic calculations and my colleague at Boston University, Paul Osterman, offered useful criticism.

Another colleague, George Lewis of the Department of Geography at Boston University, and Frederick Smith of the Graduate School of Design at Harvard helped me to get started in the study of the natural environment. Many government officials and researchers supplied data and information about Boston's current problems: Michael H. Frimpter of the United States Geological Survey, Kenneth Haag of the Massachusetts Department of Environmental Quality Engineering, Joseph McGuinn of the Metropolitan Area Planning Council Water Quality Study, David L. Rosenbloom, Commissioner of the Department of Health and Hospitals of the City of Boston, Joel Lerner, Director, Conservation Services, Massachusetts Office of Environmental Affairs and his assistant Mary Barbara Alexander. For a special analysis of the spread of zoning and the participation of towns in open land acquisition my colleague in the Boston University Law School, William E. Ryckman, gave useful guidance, and in gathering the data I was assisted by Stephen Philbin, Daniel Margolies, Eric Schneider, Hester M. Kaplan, and Alice L. Warner. Once again Eliza McClennan of the Geography Department came to my aid by drawing the very clear maps and diagrams which appear in this book.

Finally I want to thank two additional colleagues at Boston University, Cecelia Tichi of the English Department and Joseph Boskin of the History Department, for their help in thinking about the symbolic environment, and thanks also to Robie Macauley, fiction editor of *Playboy Magazine*, for his timely assistance.

SAM BASS WARNER, JR.

Boston, Massachusetts
August, 1977

I.

Slow Growth and Rapid Change

Here in New England we use our tradition of towns as a kind of shorthand description of how we live our lives beyond the threshold of our families. We identify ourselves to each other as residents of Scituate, or Wellesley, or Winthrop. The town label passes among us as a tag which tells others what sort of people we are, and what sort of life we may lead.

For ourselves the town label gives us a kind of mental snapshot of what might best be called the middle distance of our daily activity. It covers an area larger than the neighborhood, but smaller than the experience of a trip to California, or a stint in the Army or college. The town signifies to ourselves the neighbors, the children's school, the nearby friends, and some of the day's shopping and errands.

City dwellers do not lag behind in all of this. City districts have their tags—the Back Bay, Jamaica Plain, East Boston. In recent years these neighborhood labels have gained in popularity as racial conflict in the city of Boston and national wars and depressions have drained the larger political symbols of city, state, and nation of their appeal. Roxbury, South Boston, the North End, Charlestown are old names which residents increasingly employ to identify themselves to outsiders, and to interpret their own lives. Like the town labels these neighborhood tags are used as identification to strangers, for political purposes, and, most important of all, as ways of organizing personal experiences.

There is a good deal of practical wisdom in this custom. People need a way of thinking about themselves in the larger world which lies beyond the family, and the town and city district make a convenient summary of the setting of daily life with friends and neighbors.

Unfortunately, for our understanding of the world we live in, these labels do not adequately describe the way we really live. Perhaps they had more validity at the beginning of the period we want to study, the twenties, than they do now. But surely today a town or a neighborhood fails to encompass enough of our significant daily experiences to do more than offer us the false comfort that there are boundaries beyond the home which in some way define and support our lives.

Most Bostonians do not work in the towns and neighborhoods in which they live. Most Bostonians own cars, or have access to cars, and they drive them a lot: to work, for shopping, to visit friends, to see the sights, to swim or hike, to play baseball, to go skiing. Most Bostonians have a telephone at home and another at work; in neither place can the traffic on the phone be described as limited to the town or the neighborhood. Although still, for some Bostonians, the neighborhood streets, the local stores, the school, and the parish bound much of their daily lives, for most of us such limits no longer describe reality. There is reason to believe that during the twenties and thirties such limits circumscribed many married women's lives, and the lives of their children. Their lives did not even then include the scope of a man's day. If such speculations are true then the historical process since 1920 has been one in which the automobile, the telephone, and the job have enlarged the scope of women's lives even more rapidly than they have changed the experiences of men.

Now you know all this. The public does not require a professor of history to prepare an elaborate series of lectures to prove that there has been an enlargement of the browsing range of Bostonians. Weekend traffic jams on the Southeast Expressway, daily snarls on Rt. 128, the presence of big yellow MBTA busses in such unlikely places as Bedford and Concord, the seemingly endless strip of stores and restaurants along Rt. 1, the new office custom of the late afternoon phone calls to friends and relatives, are all familiar signs of a new scale to the middle distance of Bostonians' everyday life.

What you do need help with, and what we all need help with, is finding some way to comprehend this new style of life. The very fact that our middle distance is so large today, that it spills over the old town and neighborhood boundaries, makes it a life which is difficult to describe to others, or to understand for ourselves.

I wish I could say to you at the outset of these lectures that I have discovered *the* essential concept, that I had a way for us all to organize the reality of our lives, and that all you need do is sit patiently and the truth will be given to you. I have not made such a discovery, and I am therefore in the same position as everyone else in modern America. The placing of contemporary life in an accurate setting is a problem which even escapes our art and literature. Current practice is to place us all in a contrast between inner city and suburb. The device is antique. Our photographers are still going down into the city and taking pictures of people sitting on steps and playing in the streets just as Jacob Riis did in 1889. Life beyond the city is suggested by lawns, ranch houses, and backyards. Journalists and fiction writers have a greater freedom and ease in placing people in more than one setting, but they too cling to the same dichotomy. They add the inside of the city apartment to the street, and flesh out the suburbs with family-rooms and station wagons. As in the case of the town and neighborhood labels we all use, the inner-city/suburban contrast holds a measure of truth, but it is very far from the way we really live. It neither captures the complexity of our individual lives, nor identifies the uniformities which pervade many aspects of modern American living.

These lectures, then, should be considered as a kind of exercise in which we all try out varying ways of describing our lives. I will offer up descriptions of the way we all live, not just inner-city and suburban descriptions, but a whole platter full of descriptions which include everyone who can possibly be considered a Bostonian. As we examine these, what they say about life forty and fifty years ago, and what they say about life today, your task will be to formulate a description of how you live in Boston, what your middle distance is.

As a historian I insist that you think of yourself as part of historical events and processes. Without this historical effort there is no way for you to build even an approximate structure which describes your everyday experience. We all, willingly and unwillingly, participate in change. And you cannot know where you are, or where you might be going, unless you know where you've been.

I think, as a historian, I can promise you some pleasant surprises. If your experience with the material we will be dealing with is at all as mine has been, you will be surprised to learn that decisions you made in the past, decisions which you may remember as being the product of intense personal reasoning, were much like those taken by millions of your fellow Bostonians. You will also find some ways in which your life is special, unlike all other Bostonians', unique.

To begin we need some way of capturing everyone's life. The focus must be such that everyone who could reasonably be called a Bostonian does not escape our picture. Surely the people we work with, even if they commute a long way to the job, ought to be included. And the people we talk to regularly on the phone, and all the shoppers, they too must be fitted in. In short Boston must be defined as a human settlement: the place where human beings cluster together in daily activities, talking to each other, buying and selling, making things, taking care of each other, raising children, and playing. If there were some way of saying where Boston ends, and where some other settlement begins, Boston would thereby be correctly defined.

Many years ago when farms surrounded the city it was easy to say what was and what wasn't Boston. Today the stores and houses stretch out along the highway linking one town to the next so that often no clear boundary presents itself in the landscape.

A distant view of the Boston settlement will show the problem.

Some years ago the United States Air Force gave a good deal of attention to research on the nature of auroras, those streamers of light we see in the northern sky during clear winter nights. One night in 1972 the camera of a satellite was turned on to record a particularly bright aurora. By chance that same night no clouds covered the continental United States. The satellite by taking two pictures in rapid succession captured not only an extensive aurora but also the lights coming up from the land. The two pictures have been joined into one, and together they make a marvellous portrait of the human settlements of the United States (Fig. I-1).

The lights are streetlights, cars, signs—the cities and towns of the nation. Boston appears in the upper right as part of one continuous band of dense settlement which runs from Maine to Virginia. No thoroughgoing break in the light sets the boundaries of Boston for us. Yet we know that the North-

Photograph courtesy of the United States Air Force.

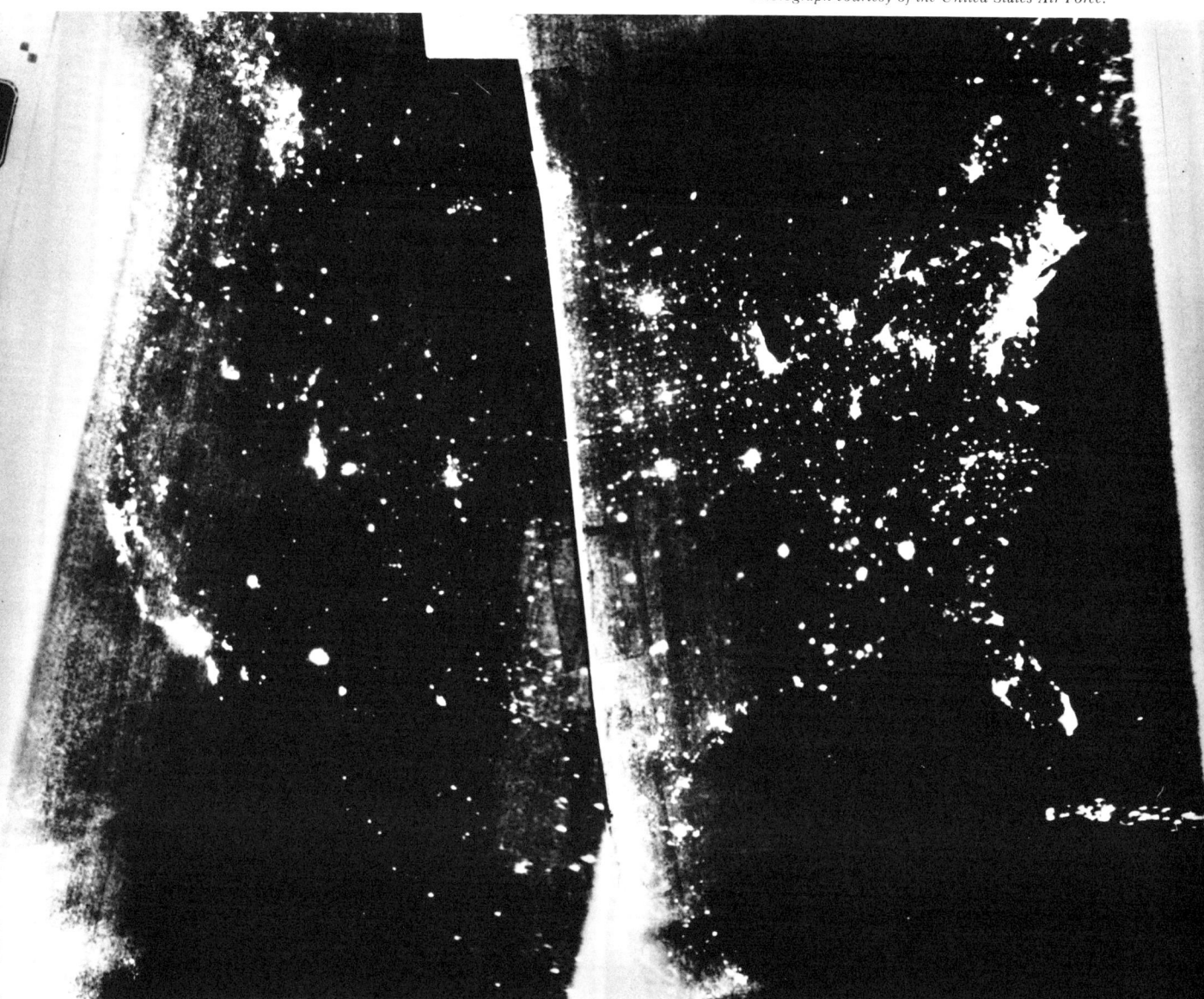

Fig. I-1
United States Air Force Satellite Photograph of the United States at Night

east Corridor, or the Atlantic Megalopolis which the satellite has picked out does not define our daily life. It is too large a space to be most people's middle distance.

A cautious viewer, one with a memory for the tricks played on the public by advertising and government photographers, might object that the night lights somehow distort the reality of life on the ground. Perhaps a daytime picture would better represent our circumstances.

An ongoing satellite program (LANDSAT) takes regular pictures of the land surface of the world,

4 THE WAY WE LIVE

Photograph courtesy of the National Aeronautics and Space Administration.

Fig. I-2
LANDSAT Infrared Satellite Photograph, North of Boston, Including Cape Ann and Southern New Hampshire

but from closer up than the aurora satellite (500 miles). It takes infrared pictures of the world that are each approximately 100 miles on a side. Here are two such pictures (Figs. I-2 and I-3) of the Boston area, roughly from Cape Cod to Cape Ann and southern New Hampshire.

To improve their clarity the original photographs were presented in false colors. Vigorous vegetation was rendered in bright red, clear water as dark blue, bare fields, roads, cities and towns in varying shades of white, gray, and light blue. Clouds remain white. In Figures I-2 and I-3, the overwhelming expanse of dark gray appears where the red vegetation was. The tiny spots and lines of light gray represent the rivers, and the cities and the towns.

Photograph courtesy of the National Aeronautics and Space Administration.

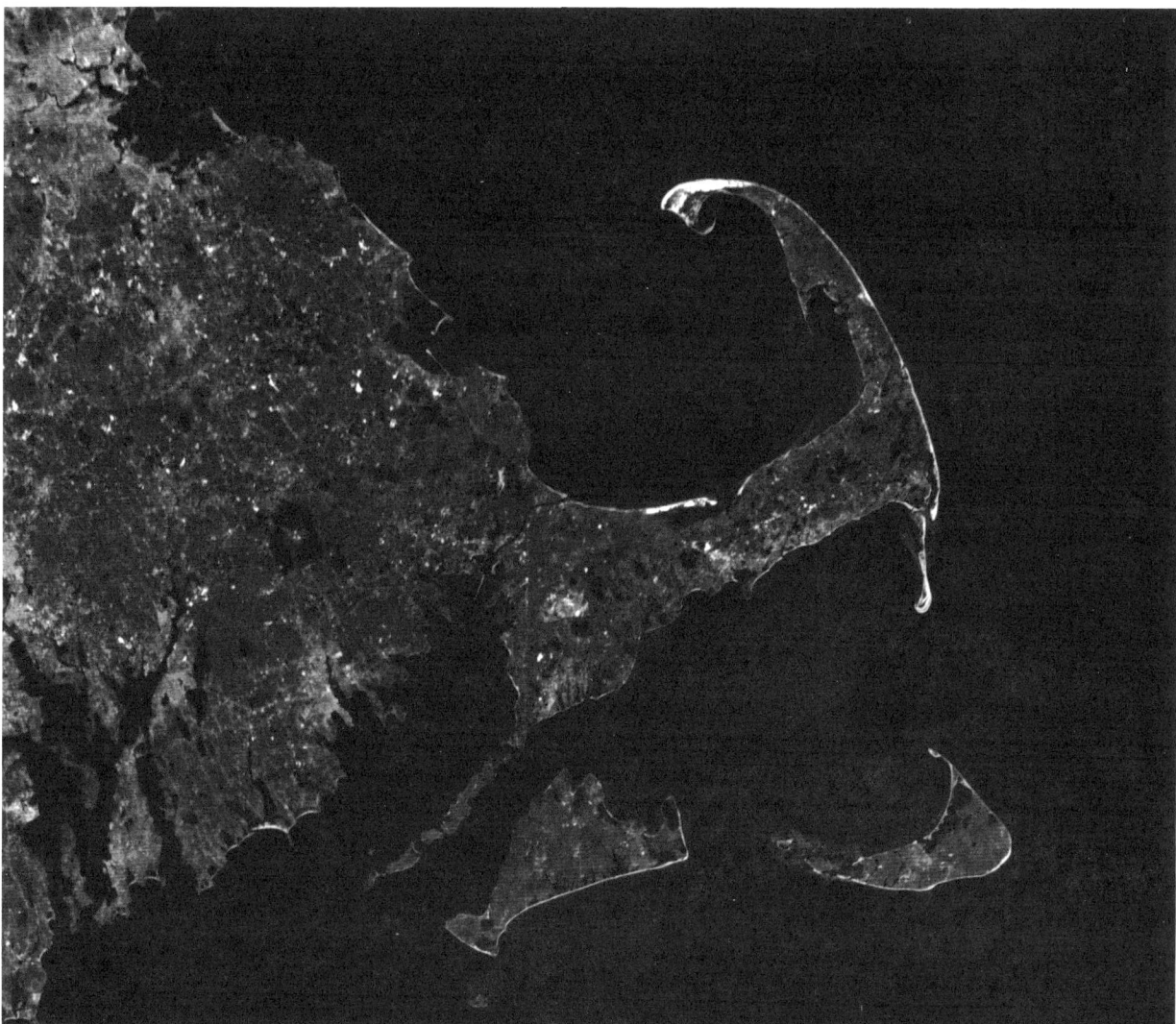

Fig. I-3
LANDSAT Infrared Satellite Photograph, South of Boston, Including Cape Cod

Now, our problem is that most of the Boston settlement has disappeared beneath the vegetation. We can locate Boston itself, some other cities and rivers, but the suburbs and small towns, all that complex daily human action we want to capture is hidden by leaves. What a strange city ours must be. This is surely not the London of Dickens, the Rome of the Antonines, or the Athens of any period.

The fact that Boston is one of the large urban areas of the world, and is mostly a city in a forest is both historically a new phenomenon and a significant aspect of contemporary American life. We will return to this issue when we examine the natural environment of our human settlement. For the moment, the wary observer's doubts deserve quieting.

6 THE WAY WE LIVE

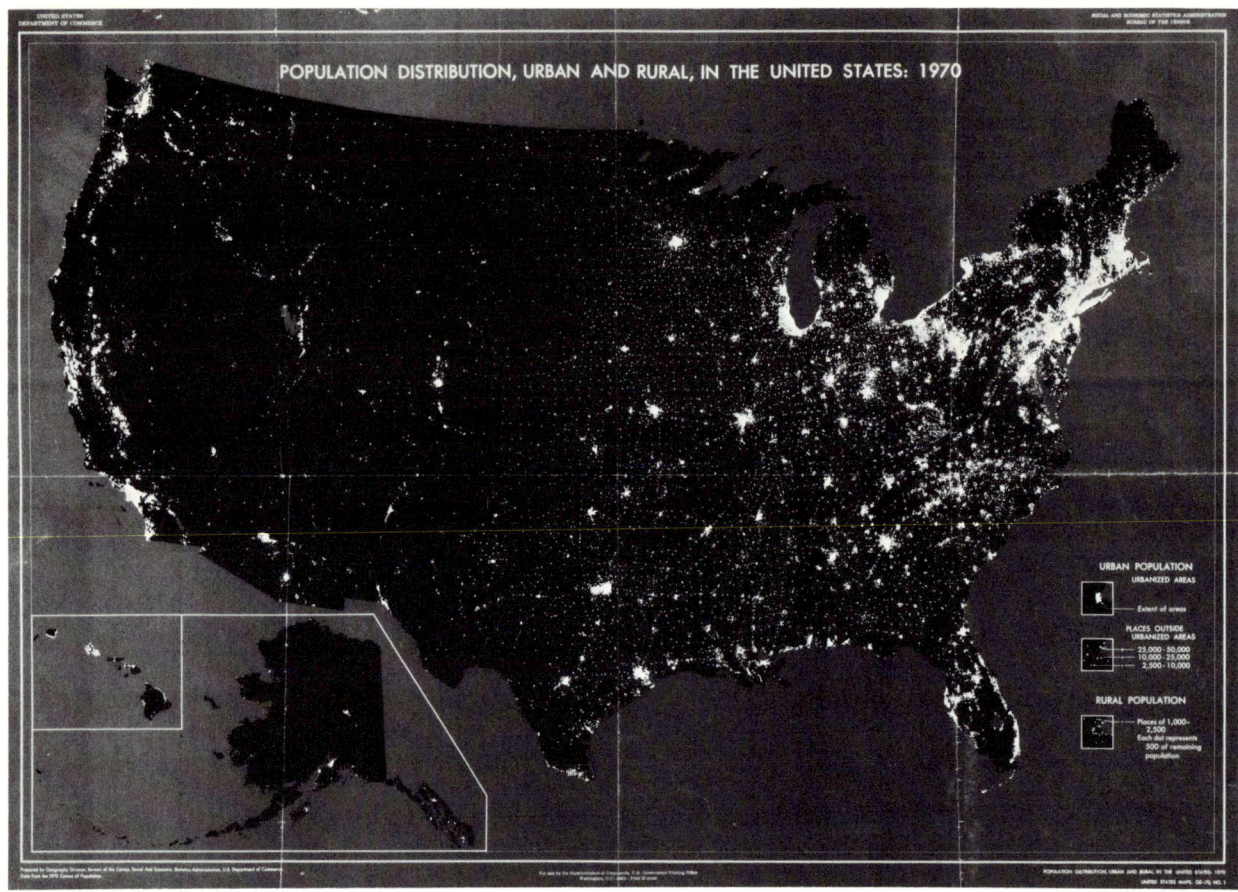

Fig. I-4
Population Distribution in the United States, 1970

Source: Geography Division, Bureau of the Census, Social and Economic Statistics Administration, "Population Distribution, Urban and Rural, in the United States, 1970."

After recording the results of the 1970 census of the United States the Census Bureau assigned a cartographer to make a map which would show the location of every American. The cartographer placed a dot on the map for each resident. His work in black and white was reversed, so that the dots show up in white and the blank spaces in black (Fig. I-4). The satellite photograph (Fig. I-1) and the Census map resemble each other remarkably well.

These four illustrations immediately tell of two aspects of our lives which we must confront. First, they tell of the enormous reach of contemporary human settlements. Second, they tell of the diffusion of settlement, a spaciousness which enables most Bostonians to live out their lives in a clearing in a forest.

A great deal of scholarly effort has been spent on the attempt to develop a meaningful definition of a city which could cope with the size and diffusion of American settlements. The Bureau of the Census wanted to organize its findings in a manner which reflected the way Americans really lived; the regional economists of the Department of Commerce needed some areas smaller than the states, but larger than the political boundaries of cities which would capture the behavior of employers, employees, and those seeking work; and scholarly geographers wanted to understand the functioning of modern urban clusters. These specialists agreed among themselves that the most promising definition of today's human settlements would come from following people in their journeys to and from work. Accordingly they added a question to the 1960 and 1970 Census which asked citizens whether they worked in the county in which they lived, or whether they travelled to another county to their job.

In New England we are not accustomed to thinking in terms of counties, our counties have few functions beyond the courts, but we are, after all, part of the United States and in most of the nation the county is a meaningful area. They can be informative units for accounting here too. The results of the 1960 Census were next compiled and analyzed, principally by Prof. Brian J. L. Berry, now of Harvard University, and by Mr. Henry L. DeGraff of the Department of Commerce.

After some years of tabulation and analysis the Census returns showed that Americans organized themselves around large central cities toward which many of them commuted each day to work. Beyond these central cities were rings of suburbs which also held many jobs. Here commuters' paths crisscrossed each other as workers travelled from one suburb to the next. Farther out still lay a very large fringe area, an area which as often as not had small cities of its own, but in which there was much less commuting toward the central city of the region. In the fringe counties the daily commuting fell off sharply until it reached a point at which residents of an outer county travelled more toward another region, and another core city. Here lay the boundary between two distinct human settlements.

The Boston area very much displays this typical American pattern. The 1970 Census returns show Boston to be a three-state, twenty-county area. Here are two maps, the one (Fig. I-5) shows the daily commuting to and from the core city, Suffolk County; the other (Fig. I-6) shows the commuting among this core and its inner suburban counties.

The preponderance of commutation to Boston comes each day from the nearby counties—104,245 from Middlesex County, 16,425 from Plymouth

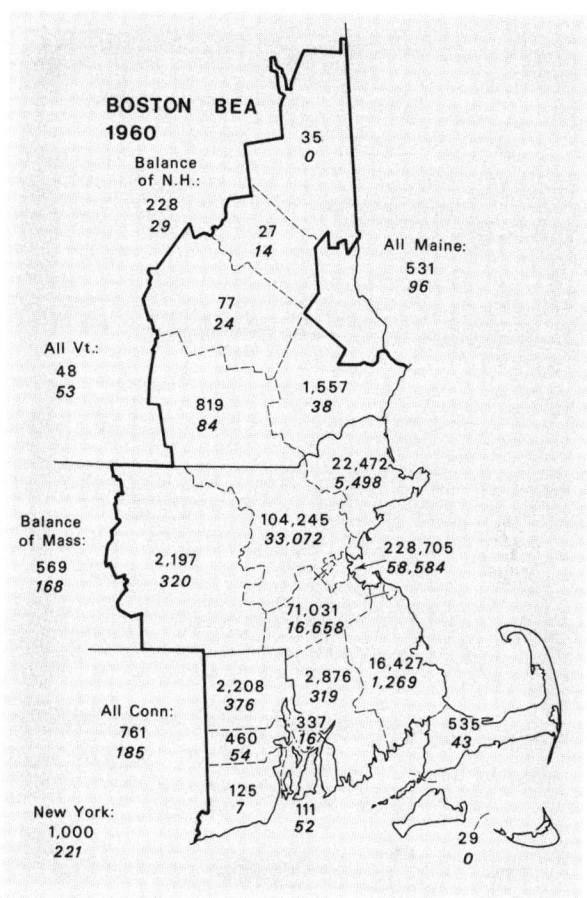

Fig. I-5
Suffolk County Commuting Patterns, 1970
999 To Suffolk County
999 From Suffolk County

Note: Net Flow to Suffolk County, 170,121.

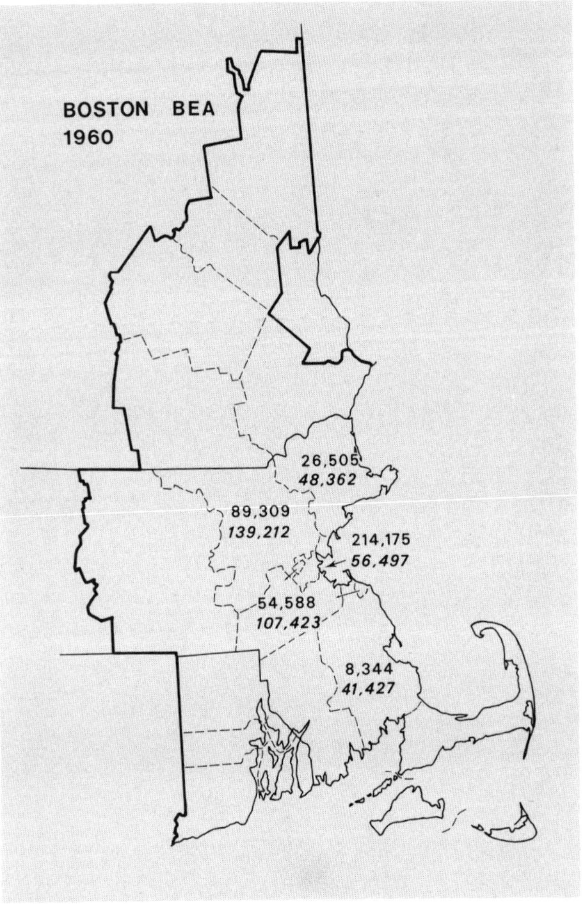

Fig. I-6
Five Inner Boston County Commuting Patterns, 1970

999 Commuters *into* a county
999 Commuters *out from* a county

Notes:
Flow among the inner Boston counties, 392,921.
Inner-county jobs equal 60.6% of all BEA jobs.
Total employed in the inner counties equals 1,428,785.

Commuters within inner counties	27.5%
Residing and working in same county	66.9
Commuters from elsewhere	5.6
TOTAL	100.0%

County, and so forth. Altogether 214,175 of Boston's 228,705 commuters come from the four inner counties (Fig. I-6, Essex, Middlesex, Norfolk, and Plymouth Counties). But there is a fringe that contributes thousands more: 2,179 journey in from Worcester County; 2,208 from Providence County, Rhode Island; and 1,557 from Rockingham County, New Hampshire.

It is possible to make such maps for every county in the United States in order to test whether any particular metropolitan grouping best represents the daily movements of Americans. Here is such a map (Fig. I-7), the record of Providence, Rhode Island. It is offered to convince you that although Providence is New England's second largest city, it has been properly included as part of Boston. Note that Providence sends more commuters out each day to Suffolk, Norfolk, Essex, Middlesex, and Worcester Counties than it receives from them. These journeys show a net flow toward Boston without any compensating flow into Providence from Connecticut. Hence Providence cannot be classified as a free-standing metropolis.

Further analysis of these commuting patterns has shown that the journey-to-work field captures within it many other aspects of a modern human settlement. The shopping paths of families also lie within the commuting range, and because newspapers, radio, and television are so oriented toward retail advertisements, their circulation and listener areas roughly coincide with the commuting field. As far as I know, complementary studies of local telephone traffic have not been made, but there is no reason to doubt that this traffic would also reveal a region with a dense center, a large outer suburban ring, and a far-reaching fringe. If you think for a moment about your own driving experience you should be able to partially confirm these findings by your own memories of traffic on the interstate highways: heavy traffic inside Rt. 128, generally easy sailing beyond.

Here then is a good answer to the boundary problem: a definition of Boston as a human settlement, a definition which captures us all at work, shopping, doing errands and visiting, reading, listening to the radio, and watching television. If the goal of our enterprise is to understand the mid-

SLOW GROWTH AND RAPID CHANGE 9

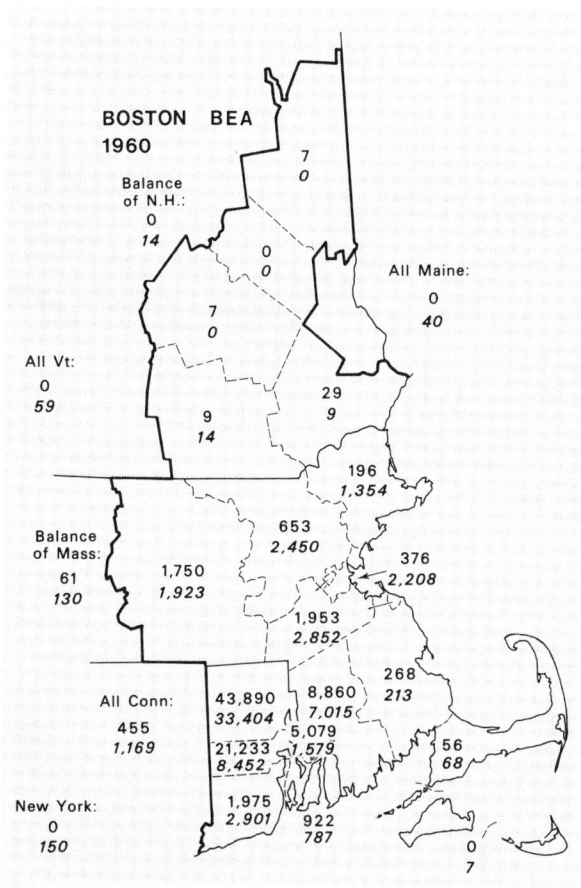

Fig. I-7
Providence County Commuting Patterns, 1970

999 To Providence County
999 From Providence County

Note: Net flow to Providence County, 11,339.

dle distance of our lives, here is where that dimension will be found.

This definition of our city has a further property which is very important to our understanding of major economic events which impinge on our lives. This Boston is a system. That is it is a gathering of interacting people and institutions. The parts connect to each other and work upon each other. If there is unemployment in Rhode Island, or New Hampshire, that unemployment affects wage levels in Massachusetts; if Boston firms cease to create new products, New Hampshire will again experience a depression; if the city of Boston goes bankrupt, its failure will weaken the credit of all the cities and towns of the region. If people now living in the inner city and suburbs move out to Plymouth, or Groton, the consequence of their new location will be shopping and services and jobs in those places, and the new jobs will form a ripple which will run through the entire region. No institution, or family, is an island within this populous region because it is a social and economic system. That's what the commonsense term "human settlement" means. Like it or not, this is our community and within it we all influence each other, and depend upon each other.

The Boston so defined currently goes by the technical name of the Boston BEA (Bureau of Economic Analysis Area). It is composed of twenty counties: ten in Massachusetts, the five counties which make up the entire state of Rhode Island, and five New Hampshire counties. Wherever possible the patterns of this metropolis will be given in terms of the BEA as a whole and for its constituent counties. Because Dukes County (Martha's Vineyard and the Elizabeth Islands) and Nantucket County (Nantucket Island) have so few inhabitants, I have combined these two into one artificial county unit labelled the Islands. Thus, our procedure will be to place the Boston BEA first in the context of the nation as a whole and then to examine what has been happening within the BEA by comparing changes in the different counties.

Viewed historically the Boston metropolis has a number of special qualities which make it an important example of American urban life. It is common knowledge among us that ours is the world's second oldest industrialized region. The wooden and brick mills yet standing beside the rivers of our towns remind us of our nineteenth-century industrial beginnings. The momentum of this headstart has long since spent itself, and in our lifetimes Boston has become a place of slow economic growth. Our economy is one of ceaseless readjustment, the death of old industries and firms, and the rise of new ones. In this respect our experience once again foreshadows the future of the nation. Slow growth, the reworking of old economies and old cities is more and more becoming *the* American situation.

Less recognized among us is the culturally advanced nature of our population. Here again Boston led the nation in low growth, not zero population growth by any means, but in a strong regional consensus that small families were the preferred adjustment to an urban and industrial world. Ever since such information began to be collected, Boston has been recorded as one of the leading regions of population control. The decline in the size of our families has been continuous since the Civil War, and when we participated in the post-World-War-II enthusiasm for children, we did so more modestly than the rest of the nation. Even overseas immigrants took up the region's ways. Although first generation immigrants tended to have larger families than the native born they did not indulge in any baby booms, and their children and grandchildren have steadfastly followed the customs of the place.

In short the consumer society was born here too, and it flourishes to this day. Compared to the rest of the United States, Bostonians, native and foreign, black and white, Protestant, Catholic, and Jew, have long preferred to buy houses, clothing, education, and entertainment, and to work less hours, rather than to put the wealth of their industrialization and urbanization into raising large families.

These two characteristics of slow growth, an economy of readjustment and a population of small families, constitute the essence of our circumstances; they pervade every aspect of our daily lives. We must understand their meaning and ramifications if we are to construct an accurate picture of the way we really live.

For some years now a political battle has been raging between the advocates of rapid growth and the advocates of slow growth. In the fast-growth camp have been businessmen and labor unions seeking subsidies and federal spending, and they have been supported by economists who cannot imagine social peace and happiness without a rapidly rising Gross National Product. In the slow-growth camp have been those fearing world overpopulation, and conservationists concerned with pollution of the environment and the waste and destruction of natural resources. The strategy of the fast-growth advocates has been to characterize low-growth societies as places of poverty and stagnation. The strategy of the slow-growth advocates has been to terrorize us with visions of starvation and natural disasters. Given the Boston experience over the past fifty years both predictions seem far from reality.

To begin with, low population growth does not mean either no change, or slow change. The Boston metropolis has been radically altered and rebuilt during the past five decades. Neither core, nor suburban ring, nor outer fringe has escaped extensive reconstruction. A single table of population change for 1920-70 tells the story (Table I-A).

This table is full of evidence of the dynamism of change which exists within a context of overall slow growth. First, note that slow growth, in past American terms at least, is still a lot of growth. The population of the Boston metropolis grew 51% in half a century. For every two people who might have lived in a town in 1920, room had to be found for another by 1970.

Second, the comparison between the Boston BEA and the United States as a whole shows the effects of population limitation and slow economic growth here. While Boston grew by 51%, the population of the nation almost doubled.

Third, the column marked Departure tells how each of the nineteen counties fared when compared to the Boston metropolis as a whole. The measure may be unfamiliar to you, but I think it is often easier to interpret than percentages which ask us to think in terms of proportions of hundreds. The departure here indicates the degree to which

TABLE 1-A

Boston BEA: Population and Population Growth, 1920-1970

COUNTY	POPULATION 1920	POPULATION 1970	GROWTH No. 1920-70	GROWTH % 1920-70	DEPARTURE
Barnstable	26,670	96,656	69,986	262.4	+56,395
Bristol	359,005	444,301	85,296	23.8	-97,652
Essex	482,156	637,887	155,731	32.3	-89,976
Middlesex	778,352	1,397,268	618,916	79.5	+222,268
Norfolk	219,081	605,051	385,970	176.2	+274,326
Plymouth	156,968	333,314	176,346	112.3	+96,355
Suffolk	835,522	735,190	-100,332	-12.0	-526,114
Worcester	455,135	637,969	182,834	40.2	-49,103
Islands	7,169	9,891	2,722	38.0	-931
Belknap	21,178	32,367	11,189	52.8	+397
Carroll	15,017	18,548	3,531	23.5	-4,122
Hillsborough	135,512	223,941	88,429	65.3	+19,372
Merrimack	51,770	80,925	29,155	56.3	+2,774
Rockingham	52,498	138,951	86,453	164.7	+59,700
Bristol	23,113	45,937	22,824	98.7	+11,046
Kent	38,269	142,382	104,113	272.1	+84,612
Newport	42,893	94,559	51,666	20.5	+51,666
Providence	474,190	580,261	105,071	22.1	-137,086
Washington	24,932	85,706	60,774	243.8	+48,069
BEA	4,200,430	6,341,104	2,140,674	51.0	-1,734,486
U.S.	105,710,620	203,235,298	97,524,678	92.3	

NOTE: Departure from BEA Norm = 1970 County Population minus BEA Population 1970/BEA Population 1920 x 1920 County Population.

SOURCE: Inter-University Consortium for Political Research, Ann Arbor, Mich.

a county's population growth, or decline, departed from the norm, the experience of the BEA as a whole. For instance, had Barnstable County grown only at the BEA average rate its departure quantity would have been zero. Belknap County, New Hampshire, with a departure of +397 almost represents a perfect average case. Barnstable County, however, grew more rapidly than the region as a whole. In fact its growth exceeded the average by 56,395 inhabitants. On the other hand, Bristol County, the area of Fall River and New Bedford, failed to grow at the average rate. Its population fell short of the average by 97,652 inhabitants.

Fourth, the variability in the county list, the large negative and positive departure quantities, indicates that although the region as a whole grew slowly, many Bostonians relocated themselves within it. Suburbs like Middlesex, Norfolk, and Kent Counties, have been popular; old mill regions like Bristol, Essex, Worcester, and Providence Counties have been relatively unpopular.

Finally, the core city itself, Suffolk County, alone in the group suffered an absolute decline in population, a loss of 100,332, and a departure from the BEA norm of -526,114. This evidence of decline in central Boston, I'm sure, comes as no surprise to you; it is the subject of every day's newscast. But stop for a moment to consider what the city of Boston would be like had Suffolk County grown at the average rate. Housing would have had to be built for 400,000 new inhabitants (departure minus net loss in population). The city would have been overrun by apartment houses. Beacon Hill and the Back Bay and South End would now be a forest of apartment towers and the single-family and two-family houses in Brighton, Jamaica Plain, Roxbury, and Dorchester would have been torn down to be replaced by six-story flats. Such a history would have relieved the strain on the tax rate, but would such a Boston be as liveable a city as the one we now have?

The changes listed in this summary table can be more easily grasped by mapping the data and by following the shifts in population decade by decade. Table I-A shows the final outcome, but we arrived at our present circumstances in two stages. The first stage lasted from 1920 to 1950. These were

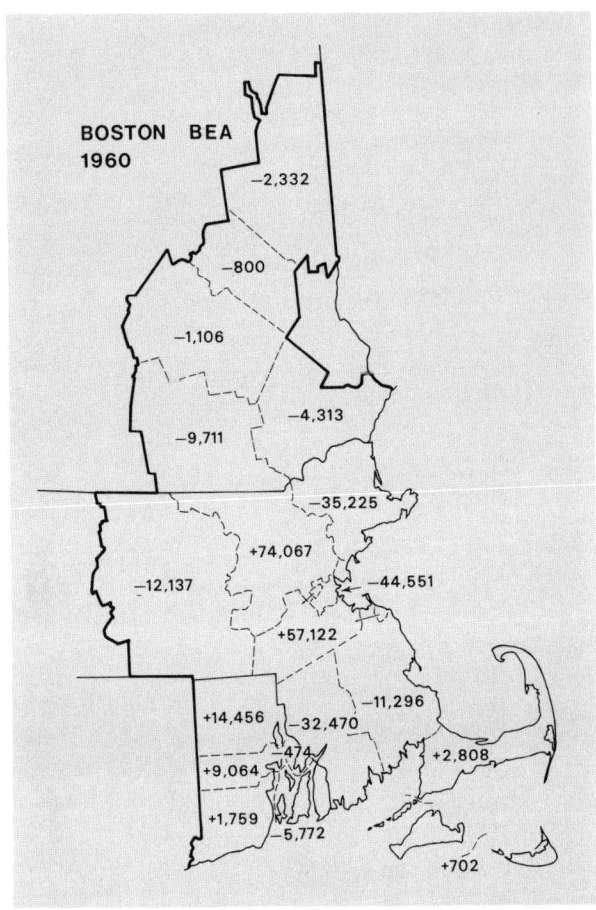

Fig. I-8
Population Shift, 1920-1930

Notes:
Boston BEA net loss equals -231,226.
Boston BEA United States growth rank, 171.
United States population growth equals 16.1%; Boston BEA growth equals 10.6%.
Intra-BEA shifts equal ±160,083.

the years of the collapse of our old mill towns and the modest growth of the suburbs around Boston and Providence. The second stage began around 1950. Since that time the suburbs have blossomed, Boston and Providence have lost ground very rapidly, and a new vitality has come to the industrial fringe both in Rhode Island and New Hampshire. Moreover, a historically unprecedented new type of fringe settlement has appeared—the retirement and resort area of Cape Cod and the Islands.

The first thing to note about the pre-World War II decades is that Boston was the slowest growing region in the United States from 1920-30 (Fig. I-8), and the second slowest from 1930-40 (Fig. I-9). The calculation of the shift away from Boston is the same departure measure as was used for the counties within Boston. The change in the Boston BEA was compared to the entire list of 171 BEA's in the nation, and the result showed a departure, or net shift away from the region, of 200,000 in each decade. More births, or more inmigration, or less outmigration would have been required to bring Boston up to the national pace. Note too that during the Great Depression Boston came close to Zero Population Growth, a decennial growth rate of only 2.4 percent. It is this historical coincidence of low population growth with economic collapse which haunts the memories of economists who press for fast-growth policies. My personal opinion is that the rate of population growth in the nation and the breakdown of the national and international economy were contemporary, but not causally related events.

The collapse of the mill economy of the Boston BEA during the twenties appears in the negative departure quantities for all New Hampshire counties and for Worcester, Essex, and Bristol counties in Massachusetts. Providence kept up to the average pace of growth during the twenties, possibly because the county included some of the city's nearby suburbs. Boston, however, began its decline in these years.

The Great Depression strongly influenced the overall rate of internal migration. When the economy failed people became trapped where they were, they were forced upon their own local re-

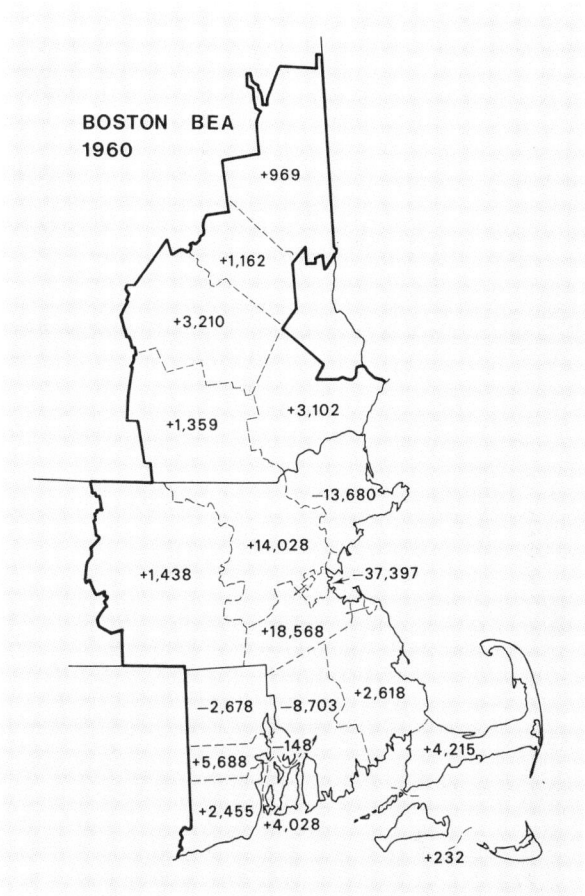

Fig. I-9
Population Shift, 1930-1940

Notes:
Boston BEA net loss equals -222,509.
Boston BEA United States growth rank, 170.
United States population growth equals 7.2%; Boston BEA growth equals 2.4%.
Intra-BEA shifts equal ±62,839.

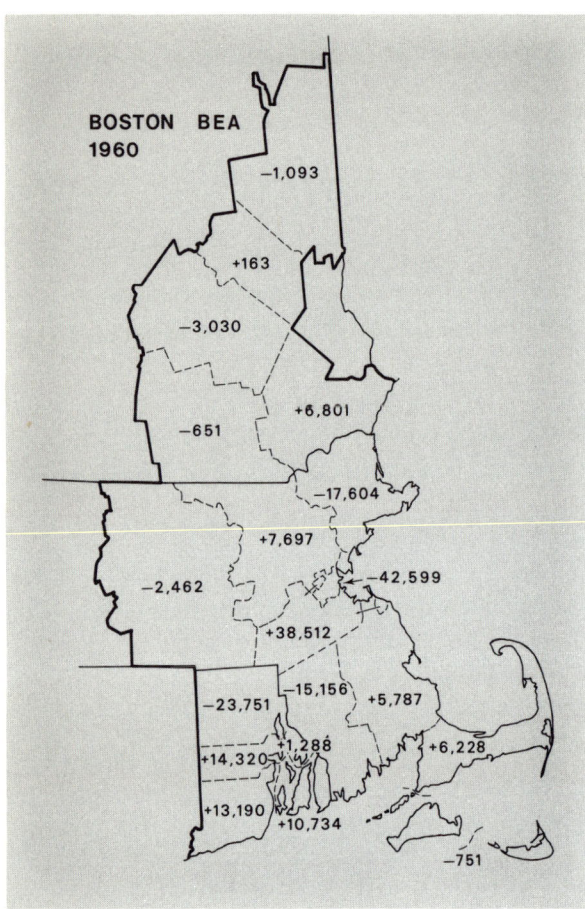

Fig. I-10
Population Shift, 1940-1950

Notes:
Boston BEA net loss equals -273,554.
Boston BEA United States growth rank, 169.
United States population growth equals 14.5%; Boston BEA growth equals 8.8%.
Intra-BEA shifts equal ±105,909.

sources and depended upon their family and friends for support. Moving from one's home base became a difficult and risky thing. The overall rate of internal migration within the BEA did not exceed the 1920's levels until 1950.

The war years show much the same pattern as the preceding decades (Fig. I-10). The region as a whole was the third slowest growing in the nation, the mill counties still failed to keep up with the metropolitan pace, and the Providence-Pawtucket-Woonsocket area joined the mill and central city decline.

Rockingham County, New Hampshire, grew at an above average rate, presumably because of activity at the Portsmouth Naval Base, and Norfolk County led in suburban growth. The resort and retirement novelty also first made its appearance with above average departure quantities for Plymouth and Barnstable counties.

Finally, note how selective the losses in population growth were becoming. The largest cities, Suffolk County and Providence County, accounted for more than half the net change in the region as a whole. This was a trend which would continue and intensify with the later diffusion of the metropolitan population.

The second era in Boston's recent population history, the era of suburbanization and the revitalization of the fringe appears in the 1950-70 population shifts (Figs. I-11 and 12).

Once again Boston continued to be one of the nation's slowest growing sections. But notice how during the wartime prosperity of the 60's the region's growth rate rose, while the national return towards small families reduced the difference between Boston and the nation (net shift 81,000).

The revitalization of the old fringe mill areas commenced. It was a change brought about in part by the possibility of distant suburban living through interstate highway commuting, and in part by the movement of new industry seeking low wages in Rhode Island and southern New Hampshire. Only Worcester County failed to achieve the BEA average, not because of economic depression and low wages, but because most of the county lay outside the suburban styles of eastern Massachusetts, Rhode Island, and New Hampshire. The

SLOW GROWTH AND RAPID CHANGE 15

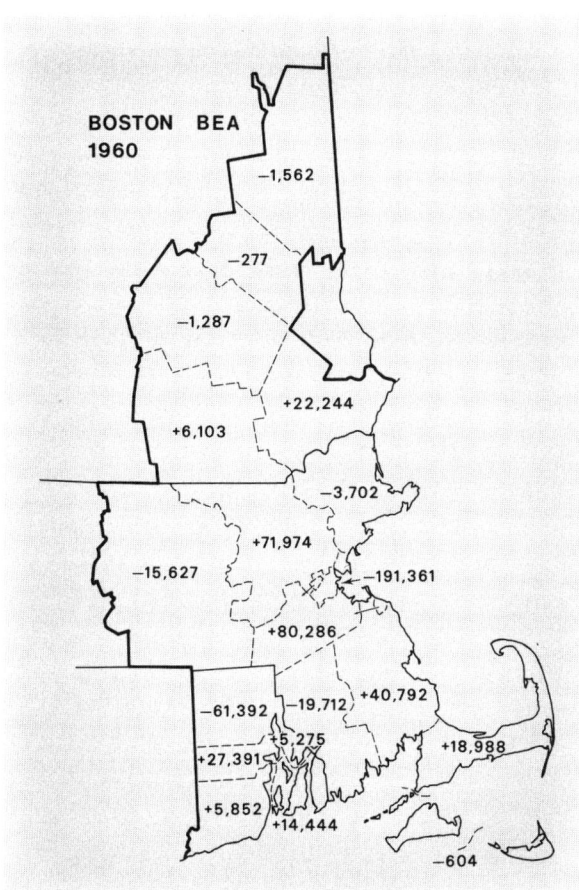

Fig. I-11
Population Shift, 1950-1960

Notes:
Boston BEA net loss equals -457,453.
Boston BEA United States growth rank, 170.
United States population growth equals 18.4%; Boston BEA growth equals 9.6%.
Intra-BEA shifts equal ±294,437.

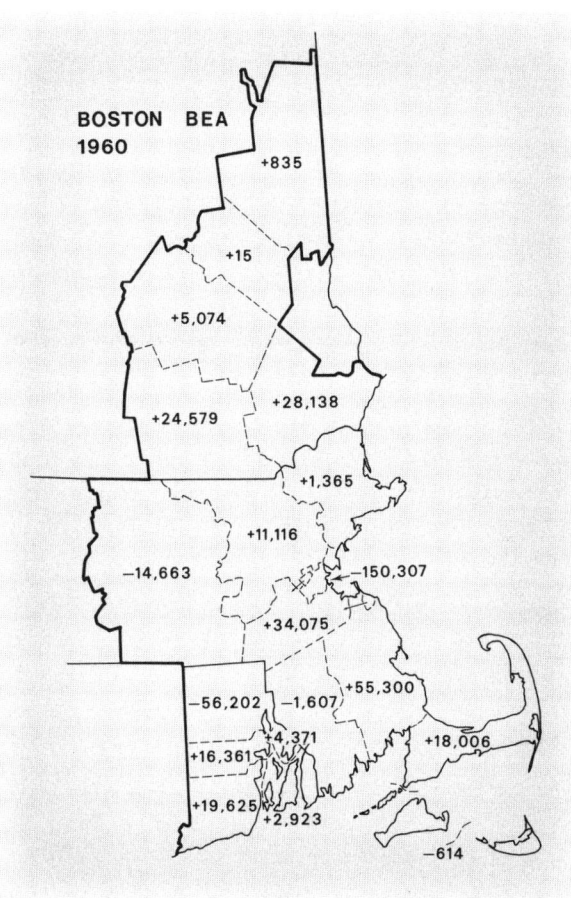

Fig. I-12
Population Shift, 1960-1970

Notes:
Boston BEA net loss equals -80,964.
Boston BEA United States growth rank, 155.
United States Population growth equals 13.3%; Boston BEA growth equals 11.9%.
Intra-BEA shifts equal ±222,588.

Cape and the Islands flourished as resort and retirement areas. This new settlement pattern is a good example of how totally unanticipated changes can take place even in the context of slow growth. No one in the twenties or thirties could have foreseen that a large segment of the Boston population would either live so long, or could afford to live out its retirement years in new homes far from their families, and far from their old neighborhoods and towns.

Finally, notice that most of the population shift within the Boston region was achieved by the relative decline of Suffolk and Providence Counties. This sort of very strong population shift is by no means historically unique. During the years from 1870-1920 rural New England emptied out and the shift was entirely towards the cities of the region. A century's view tells us of an alternation between the contraction and expansion of the metropolitan fringe population.

Given this history of a hundred-year concentration and dispersal, a few initial conclusions can be stated about our daily lives.

First, we make our way today in a settlement of enormous spaciousness. Our towns and our neighborhoods are bound up in processes of change which far exceed the political boundaries from which we derive our labels.

Second, although we know that our metropolis is, and long has been, an area of slow growth, our experience has been with a lifetime of rapid social change. Surely we should not be bullied by, or panic at, statements that urge the sudden granting of special subsidies and privileges in the name of some essential fast growth.

Finally, because our experience has been with a life of rapid change we should be modest in our projections of the present into the future. If the past is any measure of what we may expect next, we are sure it will not be what we have today.

II.

A Stable Population

Three subjects dominated the previous lecture. At the outset the issue was how to define Boston as a modern human settlement. If the goal of this inquiry was to discover how we really live in a modern metropolis, some definition was required which would capture all the people who interacted with each other daily, some boundaries that would capture Bostonians at work, shopping, visiting, talking on the telephone, and playing. The best answer seemed to be to define Boston by the range of its commuters, and that range established a metropolis of three states and twenty counties.

Second, by comparison to the rest of the nation this Boston had long been an area of relatively slow economic growth. A review of the past location of the population within the Boston metropolis, however, showed that slow growth did not mean little change. Quite the contrary. The collapse of old industries, like textiles, beginning during the 1920's meant the abandonment of mill towns at the fringe of the region. But since World War II new opportunities and new styles of living created rapid growth in the suburbs around Boston and Providence. A wholly new metropolitan district, a large resort and retirement zone, even appeared on Cape Cod and the Islands. And more recently the completion of the interstate highways and the spread of new industries have brought a return of prosperity to the fringes of the region, especially to southern New Hampshire.

Third, notice was taken of the special nature of Boston's population. For as long as records have been kept Boston has been a region of strong family limitation. We have therefore relatively less children and more adults and old people than most parts of the United States. Ours is a culture of consumers, not a culture of fertility.

These changes which have been taking place within a stable, slow-growing population deserve further exploration. Now we shall concentrate on the contribution of the family itself to the rapid shifts in the settlement patterns of the Boston metropolis. Unlike the previous lecture, and some which are to follow, there will be relatively little presentation of data on the Boston BEA. Most of our attention will be focused on long-term trends, changes going forward since the seventeenth century. To some this may appear an unnecessary detour, an excess of historical enthusiasm. For two reasons I ask that such among you be patient, and that you indulge me.

First, we must all take seriously the concept of a human settlement. We have no other moral anchor. If we are to survive, and to seek happiness in this place, the measure of our metropolis and its ways must be the measure of human life itself. Too much in this day's newspaper, or television, or academic research, employs measures far from the reference of human life. Need I repeat the truisms that cities are for man, the economy is for man, or that government is for citizens? Ironically even war itself is begun and ended in the name of some better life.

This historical excursion will, I hope, establish for us all a human measure for the metropolis so that when we come to the economy, the natural environment, and the symbolic climate, we can order these discussions in the form of two questions: what do these circumstances do for human life? what do they do for families living here in Boston?

Second, a long historical perspective is necessary because we want to explore the relationships between families and the economy and our public discourse treats the two subjects in completely different ways. The family is commonly held to be a changeless thing, the economy a hotbed of innovation.

There is an ease and detachment to our discussions about the economy. A slow-moving economy brings forth suggestions for reform as quickly as the warm spring sun brings up dandelions, and if the demands for change far exceed the changes in fact made, at least the discussion is lively and loud.

When we speak of the family, at least when we speak in public, the desperation of a people seeking certainty clouds our discourse. We speak about the family in much the same way that our forefathers discussed the gold standard—it is something immutable and self-evident, or something oppressive and immoral.

We cannot escape our deep emotional investments in the family, even if we would. Except for brief and painful moments in our lives when as adolescents we break away from our parents, or when as husbands and wives we break away from our partners, we demand certainty and stability from the family. We especially call for stability in other peoples' families. Thus, recently black families have had the exquisite pleasure of being the recipients of much public solicitude.

Therefore let us begin by loosening our conception of the family. Consider, for a moment, the word itself. Raymond Williams tells us in *Keywords* that it came into the English language from two Latin words, one of which meant servants, the other meant household. Prior to the seventeenth century the English used the word "family" in two ways. First to refer to the household—people living together, relatives and servants. The second usage is still employed—*familiar,* people one is friendly with, close to, connected to by bonds of love. Such people are one's familiars.

In the fifteenth century, Williams goes on, the term family took on an additional meaning. It was extended to include the concept of lineage, people descended from a common ancestor. The idea runs through the Bible which was at that time just being translated into English. In the Old Testament people are organized by tribes and their descent is often traced to a common ancestor, like Abraham. This practice found favor with aristocratic families whose links to ancestors worried them immensely. Ancestors were, after all, the very bread and butter of aristocrats. The old-fashioned snide remark that so-and-so is a person quite "without family" meant that a newcomer to a group lacked established and acceptable social origins. This curious usage, strange indeed for a republican people, persists today in those small pockets of the Boston metropolis where people still remember who Cleveland Amory is.

The word "family," as we commonly use it to refer to a household of a husband, a wife, and their children, first appeared during the seventeenth century and rose in popularity as this novel attitude toward one's relatives grew to be the predominant human pattern. Only in the nineteenth century did it make sense for a servant to say "the family is not at home," before then the servant was family too.

Servants used to speak of their masters and mistresses to distinguish themselves from other members of their families. So far has this trend in the use of the word "family" proceeded, that in the early years of the twentieth century social scientists were forced to invent the term "extended family" to indicate the kind of household living in which the bonds of activity and loyalty stretched beyond one common hearth.

The history of the word "family," thus, stands as a warning that whenever we appeal to this sacred concept—its collapse, its stability, or its reform—we are imputing a timelessness to what in fact has been a shifting set of human attitudes and living styles. Michael Young and Peter Willmott, in *The Symmetrical Family,* give a fine sense of the process of historical change. The authors, social anthropologists who have been studying English family life for the past thirty years, have combined a thorough survey of metropolitan London with a strong historical sense. They wrote their book with the specific goal of placing the variety of family styles which are to be found in a modern metropolis in the context of historical change.

Young and Willmott analyze all their material according to a basic concept, or model of society. They call it the principle of stratified diffusion. According to this principle social change begins at the top of a society where the well-to-do have the freedom of time and money to experiment with and to test out new fashions. If a new fashion becomes popular among the rich and powerful, then the historian or social scientist may look for later generations to take up the style as improvements in the common standard of living make imitation possible. Hence diffusion of styles is down through the classes, or strata, from top to bottom, a social process facilitated by the rising real incomes attending urbanization and industrialization. Young and Willmott's principle is the same one used by *Women's Wear Daily,* and gentlemen in the dry goods business.

For example, if one noted that in the Boston of the twenties, many Back Bay families were abandoning their city homes for their country estates in Dover or Lincoln, then one would predict that in time the middle class would abandon the city for distant suburbs. Or, if one noted that Doverites and Lincolnians were now giving up gardens and golf courses for apartments next the harbor, and for yachts, airplanes, and tropical retreats, then one might predict that some large fraction would follow them in some imitative reoccupation of the core city.

The model may be inaccurate. For a city planner or real estate man millions of dollars ride on its reliability. As a historian I think that much working-class, bottom-up, innovation went into the development of the nineteenth-century Victorian family style, but right or wrong, Young and Willmott's principle orders history into a very comprehensible form. It gives a clarity well worth borrowing.

A translation of their English history into American terms would start with a colonial nation of farmers and artisans. In this first century and a half the family was the sole economic unit and, conformable to the old meaning of the word, servants were everywhere in families—as apprentices, as indentured servants, as live-in journeymen, as farm laborers, and as slaves. The husband presided over this domestic economy as a patriarch; he determined the division of labor and he directed the tasks. Economic power and family power fused, and suffering and disaster awaited the wife, children, servants, apprentices, and slaves if their leader took sick, became a drunk, was otherwise incompetent, or died. The only social insurance to be obtained in these days consisted of well-maintained connections to relatives who could help out in emergencies.

Currently a cloud of nostalgia is drifting over these old household arrangements and some radical thinkers are calling for the return to the family as a unit of economic production. It might be well, in this context, to consider that if today you find your wife, or husband, or children a bit of a strain, imagine what it would be like if you were all shut up together in a shop or a farm. Moreover, we have in this city a slight reminder of this distant past—the relentless hours and discipline of the mom and pop stores. Or, recall our nineteenth-century novels which are filled with runaway boys, deserting husbands, and eloping girls and wives. These stories, and the perils of their heroes and heroines, stand as powerful testimony to the inflexibility of the ancient order of the American household.

The family as we look back upon it today—the household of the working husband, a domestic wife, and nonworking children, and perhaps an occasional relative—is generally described as the bourgeois family, or the industrial family. In Young and Willmott it is the Stage II family. These labels are used to mark its rise with the mechanization of farming, and the spread of cities and factories. Here in Boston, our history is the very model of such changes. The special kind of household, what we now call a family, is that very particular style of close living which is now undergoing changes, changes whose outcome is unknown to us. This uncertainty in the midst of our most intimate life is the source of much of our confusion and anxiety.

It is well for an understanding of the present not to short-circuit one's reasoning about the history of the nineteenth-century family. Scholars like Young and Willmott say it was the product of cities and industrialization. So it was, to a degree. Urbanization and industrialization made it possible for many men—but by no means all of them—to earn sufficient money to support a wife and children without their working as well. Here appeared a new social opportunity never before open to so many human beings. But surely it cannot be said that the nineteenth-century family inevitably flowered out of cities and factories. Older and alternative arrangements persisted for a very long time in the midst of this new environment.

The nineteenth-century family did not, I maintain, flow from necessity, rather it was a popular goal, something millions strove to achieve. Think, for a moment, of those sentimental cards with their sticky poetic messages which are now reprinted and sold for our amusement. They are signs of people urging each other to attempt something which did not come easily or naturally.

For the poor the new conditions did not produce a family, rather they destroyed the old household economy. The work of the poor removed to sites beyond the home. The poor sent their children out to work at an early age and, in extreme poverty, the wife worked too. The households of the poor were therefore not families at all by nineteenth-century standards, they were rooms with beds, mean cooking, and the intermittent comings and goings of household members. Such households populate nineteenth- and early twentieth-century charity and social reports. They were the "problem families" of their day, as Joseph Kett describes them in *Rites of Passage,* a treatise on adolescence in America.

Few of the benefits which accrued to the skilled workers or shopkeepers reached the poor. The husband worked long hours, he left his room early in the morning and returned late. Nor was there very much in such a household to come home to. In winter darkness even made it hard for him to see his wife, and little entertainment awaited him. The street and the saloon, those social institutions now bathed in the nostalgia of memories of the old block and the old neighborhood, offered more than the poor man's rooms, and there, outside the home, the men could be found.

Young and Willmott's earlier study *(Family and Kinship in East London)* of the life of poor working-class families in East London is a wonderfully sympathetic study of how women adapted to the harshness of such a world. Kept on a small allowance by their husbands, forbidden the income from work both by the narrowness of the economy and their culture, the wives had to make a life on their own. The English scholars' earlier study, some of which is used in *The Symmetrical Family,* shows how poor women built and maintained women's support networks in their neighborhoods. The only available resource poor wives could tap was the emotional tie between mother and daughter, and the elaboration of mother and daughter roles provided the underpinning for their mutual support and for the survival of their children.

By contrast to these harsh conditions the new life of the prosperous workingman's and shopkeeper's family had a good deal to offer that the eighteenth-century arrangements had not. These households became homes and families as we think of them when we recall our grandparents' ways. First, the household moved away from the workplace and neither wife nor children participated as producers in the economy. Then, during the latter third of the century, the home left the city for the suburbs and the power of fashion among these families completely transformed our cities. Gains in real income brought important comforts, more space in the house, running water and indoor plumbing, carpets, stoves, lights, all manner of furniture, and a varied diet.

The intensity of nineteenth-century middle-class housekeeping and its passion for objects is often a cause for wonder and ridicule among us today, but beneath its compulsion for cleanliness and fascination with the accumulation of things, stirred a battle between the family and the deteriorating urban environment which surrounded it. The cross of cleanliness to which so many women nailed themselves was the post of family survival against an appalling urban death rate. This unremitting private labor for cleanliness only became ludicrous when extensive public works at the end of the nineteenth century succeeded in transforming our cities into fit places for human life.

Much of our ambivalence about the nineteenth-century family derives from its power relationships. It is difficult for us to see behind its rules of male dominance to a time when such a state could be regarded as a goal, something for young men and women to strive toward. Like the elaborate detail of its furnishings, the hypocrisy behind its efforts at refinement and taste forbid our sympathy. After all these years I still find myself embarrassed to summon up these awful words, "refinement," "taste." Yet a refinement of manner represents one of the great achievements of the working-class and middle-class homes. We are still in debt to the efforts of these years. Their manners created the very contradictions which underpin the nineteenth- and early twentieth-century women's liberation movements.

Today we see the nineteenth-century family as a woman's prison, and so it was in a way. Isolation, dullness, routine, and unequal power between the sexes surely pervaded this home. Yet recall *Tom Jones,* or Restoration comedies, and you will be reminded of the significant benefits which Victorian manners conferred upon women. The shift from being something close to human property to being a dependent housewife protected by an elaborate code of manners was indeed a substantial improvement.

Women and children became dependents in the nineteenth century while formerly they had been producers in a family economy. But they were not partners in these earlier enterprises. They were the help, and they had the limited powers of workers and subordinates. The economic jeopardy of women and children only eased slightly during the nineteenth century, largely due to reforms in property laws, and the creation of new women's jobs in factories, school teaching, nursing, and stores. The financial uncertainty of women and children remains a problem even in our era of pensions and welfare. As most did then, so now most women must depend upon a husband for a livelihood, and if something happens to him, they must find another husband or supporting family unless they are to suffer a serious loss of income.

The new source of power for women came from the new definition of the family itself and from the woman's role within it. The whole struggle for refinement and gentility, like the struggle for cleanliness, was undertaken to set the family apart from the appalling conditions of the outside urban and industrial world. It was a world then, as the poor knew, and the middle class could easily observe, which threatened the very existence of human beings. Its morality did not include the right to a decent life.

The home and the family symbolized a striving for something better, an alternative to the behavior of the industrializing world, a "higher morality" was the nineteenth-century phrase. So far we have experienced three great waves of this sentiment, and these waves have completely refashioned our city. In the 1890's, the 1920's, and the 1950's and 1960's young families rushed to the suburbs to establish, so far as a private family could, an alternative life to that which then prevailed in the city. These family creations, of course, could only be partial worlds and it is their inevitable failings and limitations which bring us all together at the Boston Public Library to explore the metropolis our families have built.

In the nineteenth century the supervised courtship, the elaborate clothes, the taboo against vulgar language, the presumption that refined women did not smoke or use spirits, the rules of public courtesy, the innovation and elaboration of the formal parlor, the training of women in the gentle arts, all reinforced a mass search for an alternative to the crudeness and naked power of the industrial city. All these manners and customs which seem such a cloak of hypocrisy to us today, gave a new place to the woman in the home. As a special person the genteel rules offered the wife some protection against the physical violence of her husband, how much protection no historian can estimate. My guess is more protection than in the eighteenth century.

While the poor wife depended upon her neighborhood network for support against her husband and the vicissitudes of his life, the middle-class matron steadily gained control over her family's social life. Custodian of the family's social position, she set its visiting patterns and even some of its institutional connections. The wives seized the churches, and from their church victory they moved on to charity and social reform, and a few even to women's politics.

Finally, in the shift from household worker to genteel housewife, women gained sexual power. The prudery of the Victorian age confounds us in these times of sensuality and sexual thirst. The openness of the sexual code of Ben Franklin's day is more to our taste. But in formal rules, in delicacy, fainting, vapors, and all the neurotic folderol of the Victorian code lay power—the power to refuse, or at least to temporize. The eighteenth century had a double standard of sexual behavior for men and for women, so did the nineteenth, but the later one at least increased the married woman's sexual bargaining power at home.

These wives were after all the women who seized upon the consumer culture. At the end of the century the wealthiest among them sometimes spent days at a time shopping in department stores. They were the women who sharply limited the size of their families; they sent their daughters to high school and later to college. Their goals for their children were not to labor in the family business, or even a better factory, or a nicer farm.

Although the roles assigned by the nineteenth-century family are under constant barrage, that century's idea of a household restricted to the emo-

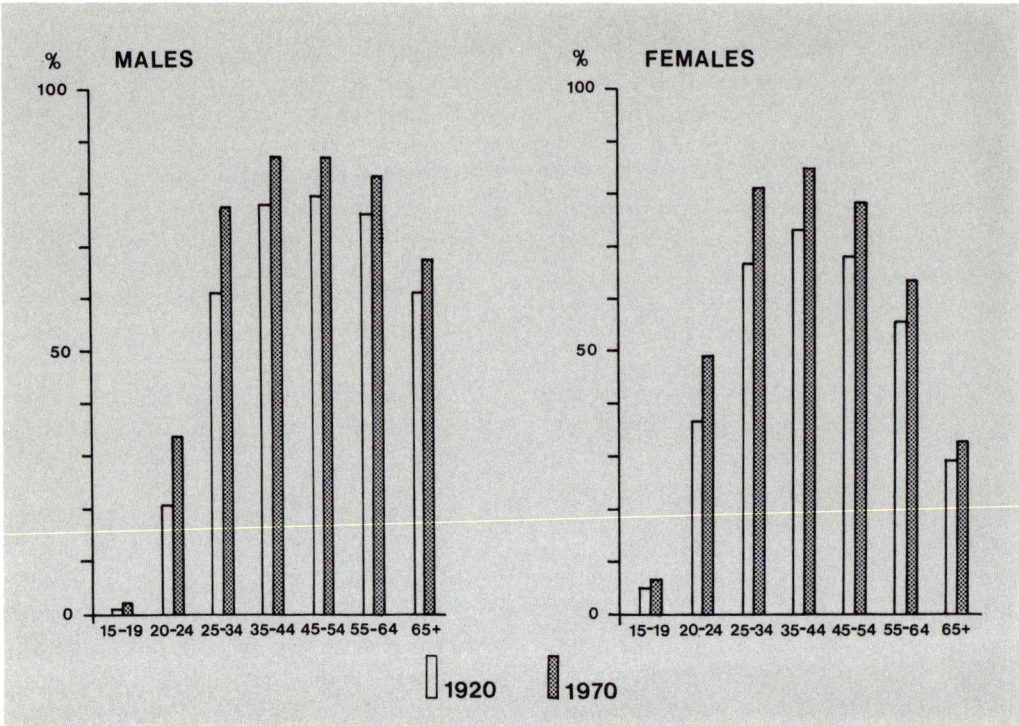

Fig. II-1
Population Fifteen Years and Older, Married, Tri-State Area, Percent
Source: 1920 United States Census, Table 11; 1970 United States Census, Table 152.

tional network of a husband, a wife, and their children has reached new heights of popularity. The latest census gives only 1970 data, and surveys indicate there has been some falloff in the family ratings since then. Still, marriage here in Boston exceeds its 1920, and even more its 1890 levels. The accompanying chart (Fig. II-1) shows that for both sexes, and at all age levels, people are marrying more than they used to back in 1920.

A curious asymmetry prevails in the marital status of men, as opposed to women. Although we seem to believe that living as couples is a wonderfully desirable state, and although we limit the number of our births, and concentrate them in the early years of marriage, we behave between the sexes as if fertility were our goal. Note on the chart, that in the age groups after 44, a much higher proportion of men are married than women. The disparity came about because men die younger than women, and because when a man loses or leaves a wife, he reaches down into the age pool of younger women to find a new bride. As a result there are many more leftover women than men. Such an imbalance is appropriate for a patriarchal society, one concerned with the multiplication of children and domestic animals, but surely it is unseemly for a society seeking zero population growth, and one which wants to promote living in couples.

This sex imbalance came about because both the economy and the symbolic climate of the nation fostered the image of women as girls and the image of men as fathers. If these images were reversed so that the desirability of women derived from their motherly qualities, and the desirability of men from their boyishness, then women would marry men younger than they, and sexual symmetry in the years after 44 could be attained.

Perhaps these are frivolous speculations. But note how these simple marriage statistics lead to the heart of our way of life.

Table II-A is a detailed listing of the 1970 percentage distribution of family types in Boston, county by county. If you read sideways, adding the percentages for one county the total will be 100 percent. That is, the sum of the husband and wife families, and the single-headed female families, and the single-headed male families equals all the families in a county.

The BEA summary line is the best place to start because it gives a measure for interpreting the county data. The variations in the proportions of husband and wife families with and without children under 18 arise from the differing concentrations of old people in our metropolitan region. Barnstable County and the Islands, Belknap and

TABLE II-A

Composition of Families, 1970

(Percent Total Families)

| | HUSBAND & WIFE FAMILIES | | SINGLE-HEADED FAMILIES | | | |
| | | | *Female Head* | | *Male Head* | |
	with child under 18	without	with child under 18	without	with child under 18	without
Barnstable	40.5	46.9	5.5	4.9	0.6	1.7
Bristol	46.6	38.5	5.7	6.3	0.6	2.3
Essex	48.0	37.6	5.1	6.3	0.6	2.4
Middlesex	50.2	35.9	4.4	6.5	0.6	2.4
Norfolk	51.1	36.4	3.8	6.0	0.6	2.1
Plymouth	53.7	33.9	5.2	4.8	0.6	1.8
Suffolk	37.4	36.5	10.7	10.7	0.8	3.9
Worcester	48.2	38.2	4.8	5.9	0.6	2.4
Islands	40.5	45.0	4.7	6.7	0.6	2.5
Belknap	46.5	41.8	4.4	4.5	0.8	2.0
Carroll	41.4	47.2	4.2	4.2	0.9	1.9
Hillsborough	51.9	36.0	4.4	5.0	0.7	2.0
Merrimack	48.1	39.9	4.7	4.7	0.8	1.9
Rockingham	53.2	36.9	4.2	3.3	0.7	1.6
Bristol	53.2	36.0	3.6	5.0	0.5	1.7
Kent	51.7	37.4	4.0	4.3	0.6	2.0
Newport	47.5	35.6	9.6	4.8	0.7	1.9
Providence	43.3	40.2	6.0	7.1	0.6	2.8
Washington	51.0	35.9	7.2	3.8	0.6	1.4
BEA	47.7	37.3	5.5	6.5	0.6	2.4

SOURCE: U.S. Census: 1970, Tables 36, 37.

Carroll counties in New Hampshire, and to a lesser extent Bristol County, Massachusetts, and Providence, Rhode Island, hold disproportionate numbers of old people, and hence many childless couples. Conversely, the new concentrations of young families in Plymouth County, Massachusetts, Hillsborough and Rockingham Counties in New Hampshire and Bristol County, Rhode Island show the opposite tendency.

Current anxiety about the family, however, does not arise from these distributions, but rather from the incidence of family dissolution. In metropolitan Boston 15% of all the families are single headed; 6.1% of our families are single-headed families with children under 18. Exactly comparable data for the 1920's is not available, but if one takes into account the difference in the life expectancy of 50 years ago there can be no doubt that the incidence of broken families is at its historic peak. Thus, our situation is one in which more and more people are trying marriage, and an ever higher proportion of those trying are not finding it to their taste.

All the counties in the region, suburban and fringe alike, have a 10 to 12% distribution of broken families, but there are a few spots where single-headed families concentrate. Suffolk county stands far above the regional average with more than one quarter of its families single headed (26.1%).

Two distinct conditions combine to make this high proportion. First, Suffolk County contains most of the entire region's black families, and the black family has dissolved in America's northern cities. Nationally, according to the Bureau of the Census, the proportion of ever married females who are divorced or separated at any one time is 9.8% of all white females (25-54) and 31.0% of all black females. Suffolk County may also be a place where the divorced and separated congregate in the hope that centrality will help them find another partner. The same forces seem at work in Providence County; while the high incidence of female-headed families with children at Newport is probably the result of the behavior of Navy personnel.

These single-headed families are of several types. In many of those without children under 18, death has removed the husband or the wife. Others are remnants of childless divorced or separated couples.

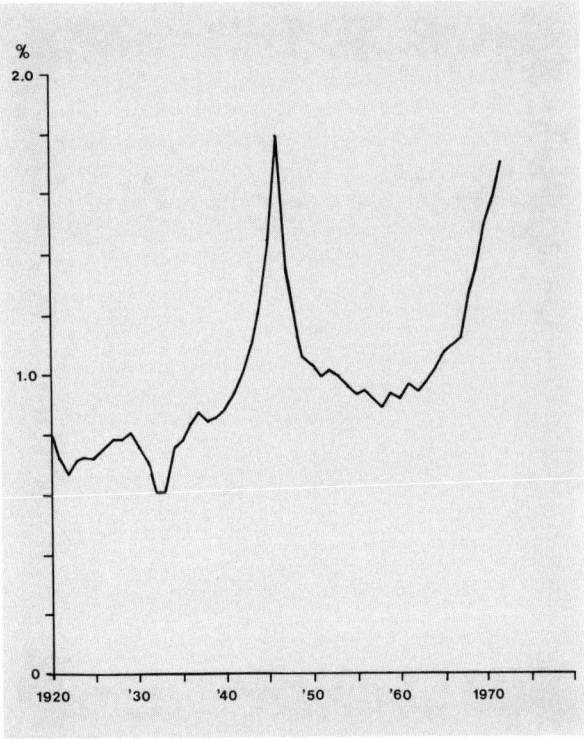

Fig. II-2
Annual Rate of Divorce Per One Hundred Married Women Fifteen Years and Older, United States, 1920-1972

Source: Department of Health, Education and Welfare, National Center for Health Statistics, *Vital Statistics of the United States,* 1972, Vol. 3, Table 2-1 (Divorces and Annulments).

The twentieth-century postponement of death has been a great gift to family life and this component in the data on single-headed families is probably lower than ever before in history. The turmoil about childless couples perhaps also should be dismissed as an issue of no public concern—it is the cost of a society of choice undergoing a change in its goals and attitudes.

The single-headed families with children under 18, are, however, a matter for public concern. From a child's perspective it seems as if medicine had rescued him from the nineteenth-century world of widows and orphans only to deliver him into a twentieth-century world of divorcing parents. In

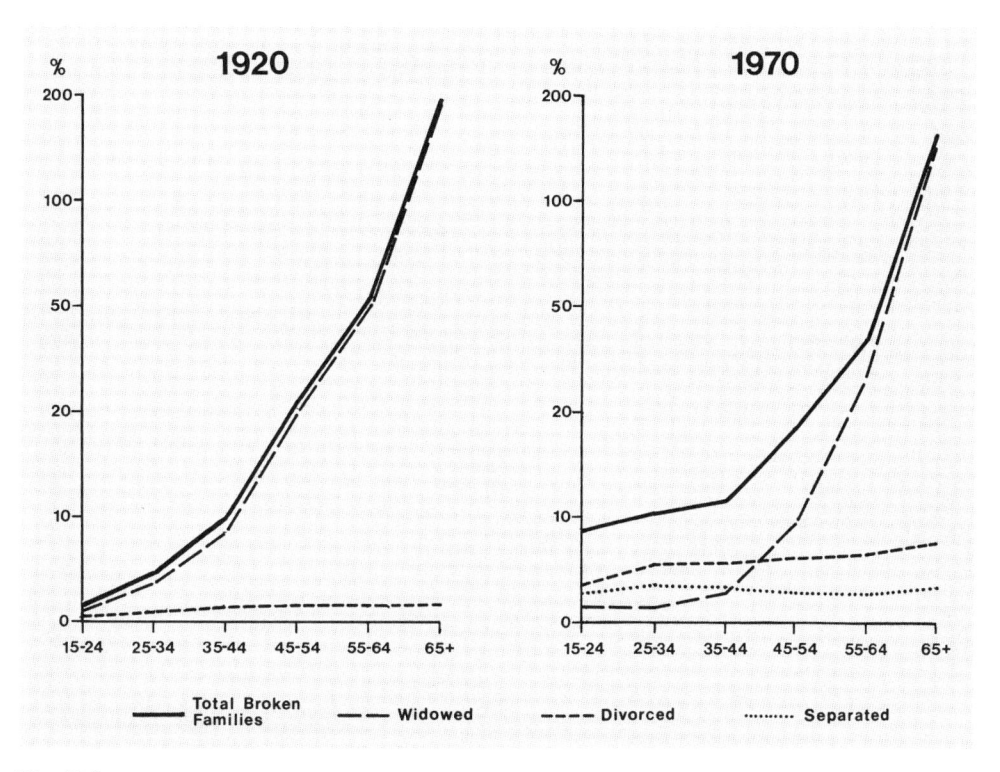

Fig. II-3
Women in Broken Families Per One Hundred Married Women Fifteen Years and Older, Tri-State Area, 1920 and 1970

Source: 1920 United States Census, Table 11; 1970 United States Census, Table 152.

1970 within the Boston metropolis 96,000 single-headed families were raising 210,000 children. Since nine tenths of the families are female-headed they face the financial hardship of a society which pays men at about twice the rate of women. Moreover the creators of the social security and welfare system had the nineteenth-century family in mind when they wrote this basic family legislation, and it ill suits our current behavior.

These families' lack of human resources is as dangerous as their lack of economic power. Every parent knows that four hands make it easier to raise up children than two. Studies of children's behavior and development seem to indicate that children fare better growing up in a household with two adults of opposite sex than in living with one parent. I offer no solutions to this situation; it is one of the major social problems of our metropolis.

The divorce rate itself teaches an important lesson about our behavior. Although we all have a vested interest in family stability, and although government officials, city planners and businessmen could reap enormous benefits from knowing ahead of time how the population was going to change, nothing in recent years has been more impossible to predict than trends in demographic statistics. Figure II-2 shows the national divorce rate for the United States. Keep in mind that a one percent annual rate, if no one ever remarried, would produce after one decennial census a ten percent proportion of single-headed families.

A final chart (Fig. II-3) will show what has been happening to us all since 1920. In that year, as in the decades previous to it, the major cause of the dissolution of families was death. Since 1920 divorce and separation have risen to be major causes in their own right. In Figure II-3 compare the 45-54 age group in 1920 with the same group in 1970. One quarter of the married women in 1920 in that age group were without husbands; almost all were widowed. In 1970 only 18% of that group had lost partners, and divorce and separation accounted for almost half the broken family losses. The overall thrust of historical change has been, thus, from a time when families were threatened by death, to a voluntaristic society where the partners themselves chose to stay together or to break up.

The contrast between this chart of women in broken families and the earlier chart of marital status summarizes our current predicament. More of us, men and women, are trying marriage than our parents or grandparents' generations did. But we seem not to know what we are seeking.

Our families are liberated for a long span of years from the fear of death of one partner, yet the concept and goals of the family itself are unclear. After experiment many of us find the alternative of a fresh start, or a single life, better than the families we form.

We started this lecture looking for a simple obvious human measure for our metropolis, its economy, its environment, and its symbols. Surely the condition of families ought to be a leading social indicator of the health of our urban world. Yet our family situation is thoroughly ambiguous.

A nineteenth-century workingman could say with conviction that he should be better paid so he could pursue a decent family life: he knew what that life ought to be. We are not in his position. Surely our goal ought to be to build a metropolitan economy and a metropolitan society which will sustain family life. But, we do not at present know what that family life ought to be.

III.

The Family and the Metropolitan Economy

The world I live in as an academic is deeply divided between those who seek reality in numbers and in carefully defined logical constructs, and those who seek reality in language and the suggestive power of verbal formulations.

To the extent that you live in the business and institutional world of Boston your life is divided between the reasoning of the job and the reasoning of the home. Your division does not suffer from the traditional intellectual separation of the academy. In both your life spaces all ideas are welcome so long as they can prove themselves in the short-lived world of practice, so long as they work.

In business the most bizarre and lethal science is acceptable if it will make electricity, if it imitates the latest art vogue, if it will sell perfume. The sloppiest psychotherapy is seized upon if it makes some people feel better.

Your practical world suffers not from formal barriers to ideas, but from divided purposes. What works in business and everyday affairs is what makes the institution grow and prosper. What works at home are those things which bring immediate profit and happiness to the family. The fact that in our business and government roles we attack our lives as families, or that as families we seek private gain at the expense of all our neighbors, is the moral division we have all learned to cope with.

Neither knowledge, nor the success of a modern human settlement requires such extreme psychological separations; they are our traditions, not our necessities. Indeed we can all prosper together only if these divisions are broken down.

In the first lecture we started with a commonplace experience, living in a modern American city, Boston, and aided by the latest machinery of science, the computer and the earth satellite, we came to define that experience as being bounded by three states. In the second lecture we began with the universal experience of family life, and employing the methods of academic letters, the *Oxford English Dictionary*, and the writings of historians, showed our contemporary conflict and changing expectations to be the product of long historical processes which reached back at least to the seventeenth century. Thus, by travelling both paths, the path of science and the path of letters, we have learned that our lives in this modern American city are much larger in space and much longer in time than we ordinarily think them to be.

The great spatial and temporal expanse of contemporary life, however, is no excuse for ignorance. Unlike those that came before us we have sufficient accumulated knowledge, technique, and equipment to create accurate descriptions of the way we live.

It is my belief that many of the destructive, indeed self-destructive, aspects of our human settlement come not from iron necessities, but from our unwillingness to confront what we as a society know about ourselves. The computer technician does not set his machine to the urgent tasks revealed by the novelist or the politician, and these gentlemen do not take the time even to read the social portraits the computer draws. The rationality and universality of business and government are kept separate from the wisdom of home and community, while the fellowship and emotional richness of these domestic worlds are not regarded as acceptable measures of business and public life.

In this and succeeding lectures I will try to demonstrate how these traditional barriers can be bridged. You may remember that we found some common-sense validation of the abstract computerized definition of Boston in our automobile driving experience. Conversely the statistics of marriage, households, and divorce confirmed the literary evidence which our history of the family rested upon.

In this and the next lecture, we shall take up the metropolitan Boston economy, its past and its present problems. To bridge across the worlds of numbers and letters, to force family to confront business and government, we shall describe the economy simultaneously in the concretions of family life, and in the abstractions of academic economics. I mean by this merging of disparate perspectives to state that we should be willing to apply our family experience and values to our economic affairs, and that we should apply all our modes of knowledge to the problems of living together in the vastness which is a modern metropolis.

TABLE III-A

	THE WHITES		THE BLACKS		THE SILVAS	
1920, Singles:						
Age 24	Michael	$ 2,392	Sam	$2,303	Manuel	$2,176
Age 22	Maureen	1,644	Malvina	1,390	Annette	1,521
1922, Marriage:						
	Michael	3,094	Sam	2,581	Manuel	2,820
	Maureen	1,979	Malvina	1,390	Annette	1,637
		5,073		4,206		4,457
1926, First Pregnancy:						
	David Born		Ronald Born		John Born	
	Michael	4,500	Sam	3,138	Manuel	4,107
	Maureen	2,630	Malvina	2,094	Annette	1,868
		7,130		5,232		5,975
1928	Mary Born		Georgia Born		Jeanne Born	
1930	Michael	5,904	Sam	3,694	Manuel	5,394
	Maureen at home		Malvina at home		Annette	2,100
						7,494
1936, Thinking of Splitting Up:						
	Maureen could earn	3,200	Malvina could earn	2,871	Annette is earning	2,280
1942, Youngest Child 8th Grade, Wives Return to Work:						
	Michael	8,269	Sam	4,325	Manuel	6,446
	Maureen	3,355	Malvina	3,194	Annette	2,550
		11,624		7,519		8,996

Table III-A presents a scenario for three average Boston families. The scenario has been built from estimates of the 1920-1970 economic histories of all Bostonians in the BEA. The family earnings differ from each other because men earn different wages than women, because whites earn different wages than blacks, and because work in some industries, like manufacturing and public utilities, is better paid than work in retailing and services. The family earnings also differ because two of the families live at the center of the metropolis where wages are the highest, and one family lives on the fringe, where wages are always lower.

TABLE III-A

A Scenario for Three Average Boston Families, 1920-1970

The Whites, the Blacks, and the Silvas were all born in the same years, all were native Bostonians, all were successful workers whose share of layoffs, wage cuts, and overtime was the same as the national average for their industries. Their income experience is that of the current (1973) Boston metropolis projected backwards according to past national trends. All figures in the table which follows are given in constant 1974 dollars, not in the wages of the past. They are thus adjusted to reflect real income. All income is listed as gross income *before* taxes. Finally none of the families are assumed to have

TABLE III-A *(continued)*

1947 The Whites buy a house, the Blacks buy a car, the Silvas buy a two-family house with the aid of their parents who take the downstairs apartment.

1950, The Golden Years:

	Michael	9,471	Sam	5,002	Manuel	7,371
	Maureen	4,089	Malvina	3,666	Annette	3,148
		13,560		8,666		10,519

1950, Children Out on Their Own:

Age 24	David	4,070	Ronald	4,178	John	3,689
Age 22	Mary	4,037	Georgia	2,903	Jeanne	2,759

David works for the telephone company, Mary in a store on Newbury Street; Ronald is in a big insurance company, Georgia works for the Gas Company; John is an accountant, Jeanne is employed by a local bank.

1960

	Michael	$10,414	Sam	$5,372	Manuel	$6,042
	Maureen	4,632	Malvina	3,817	Annette	3,390
		15,046		9,189		9,432

1960, The Children:

Age 34	David	10,761	Ronald	6,607	John	7,275
Age 32	Mary	6,447	Georgia	4,749	Jeanne	3,234

1970, If Working Instead of Retiring:

Age 74	Michael	8,476	Sam	6,267	Manuel	6,070
Age 72	Maureen	3,911	Malvina	3,038	Annette	3,073
		12,387		9,305		9,143

1970, The Children:

Age 44	David	15,968	Ronald	8,331	John	10,926
Age 42	Mary	6,954	Georgia	6,746	Jeanne	4,809

moved out of their counties, or the workers to have changed their industries, during their lifetimes.

In thinking about the significance of this scenario it would be helpful to remember two things. First, these calculations are based on average earnings. In the United States, the average earnings figure always lies above the median so that more families in Boston earned *less* than the scenario families, rather than more. Second, the Bureau of Labor Statistics in recent years has maintained cost-of-living budgets for the cities of the United States. For the Boston SMSA in April, 1975, its lower budget was $9,200, its intermediate budget $14,300. Both budgets assume a settled family headed by an ex-

perienced worker aged 38, a nonworking wife aged 36, and two children, a boy 13 and a girl 8.

The lower budget allowed for a rental unit with the tenant paying for utilities and insurance on his personal property (total housing cost $1,758), Blue Cross and Blue Shield medical insurance, and a six-year-old car which was to be traded in every three years. The social security and personal income taxes (the sales taxes are absorbed in the estimates of purchased items) totalled $1,463.

The intermediate budget allows for a home, purchased six years ago, its taxes, mortgage, maintenance, heat, etc. (total cost $3,236), a two-year-old car purchased every three years, Blue Cross and Blue Shield and ex-

The dollar figures of the past have all been translated into equivalents for today's paycheck (constant 1974 dollars), so that anyone can compare his situation with the conditions of the past. It might be well to note that this concretion is only possible because the data, indices, and concepts behind the estimates were painfully assembled and interpreted through fifty years of labor by arcane academic and government economists, the very type of people scorned by the man of affairs and the stylish humanist.

This table of family earnings raises most of the basic issues about the performance of the metropolitan Boston economy during the past half century. Begin with the successes. Family earnings in all cases rose from the early years to the worker's mid-fifties. Here is where our overworked slogans find their justification—"the land of opportunity," "the rising standard of living," and "the growth economy." No matter who you may be, with a little luck and perhaps some willingness to change employers, when you are middle aged you can look backward to see material progress.

TABLE III-A Scenario *(continued)*

tended hospitalization insurance, and personal income and social security taxes of $2,790.

The Whites and the Blacks both live in Suffolk County. Michael White is a machinist, his wife Maureen Sullivan is a registered nurse; Sam Black works in a shoe factory, his wife Malvina Brown is a licensed practical nurse. The Silvas live in New Bedford, Bristol County. Manuel Silva works in a retail store, his wife Annette Michaud is a textile factory worker.

Formal Assumptions: All data are projected backwards from the 1973 Social Security Continuous Work History 10% Sample for Counties nonmigrant workers. The variations among the Boston counties, and the differences in income according to sex, race, and age, are assumed to have remained in the same proportions in the past as they do now in 1973. The differences in industry experience are estimated according to the national industry group averages given in *Historical Statistics*, vol. 1, Tables D739-764. Past earnings levels were converted to constant 1974 dollars according to the implicit price deflators for the Gross National Product given in Tables E 1-22.

This perspective view is a composite, the blurring together of our social tradition of an age-graded wage scale and the economic achievement of rising productivity for workers and management. Our tradition, a social usage much more than the rewards of efficiency, demands that young people be paid at beginners' wages and that as one gets older, regardless of whether one gets wiser, more responsible, more skilled, or more effective, one gets paid more. In the Boston BEA today, according to the United States Department of Commerce, average wages begin at a low level for people in their twenties, rise rapidly to a peak during the years 35-44, and then fall off slowly. The 20-24-year-olds earn 56% of the peak age group, the 50-year-olds earn 84% of the peak, and the 60-year-olds earn 71% of the 35-44 age group.

But notice in Table III-A, no appreciable fall-off in earnings takes place among these average families until they are seventy years old. Instead they experience gains in all decades through their sixties. No earlier peak occurred because the decline in their earnings was forestalled, indeed reversed, because they, like other Bostonians and most Americans, were riding the elevator of rising real income. Throughout their lifetimes the improved productivity of the economy brought their families rises in real income decade by decade (with the possible exception of the 1930's), and these increases offset the up and down increments of the age-graded wage scale.

The evidence of real-income gains stands out most sharply in a comparison between parents and children. The sons and daughters working in their thirties and forties earned about twice what their parents did at the same ages in their lives. To say that real incomes of Americans and Bostonians had increased two-and-a-half times since 1920 would be an adequate approximation of the general improvement in the productivity of our economy.

This substantial improvement in the material conditions of Americans is surely an important justification for our mixed capitalist and public economy. It has for a long time made everyone richer; as an economy it produces; it works.

But perhaps we congratulate ourselves too much. The rate of growth may be too slow, slower than it might have been if another type of economic organization had prevailed. Or, perhaps the rate is too fast, too much of the future in terms of both natural resources and human lives was consumed in this rush towards added productivity.

The science of economics does not offer any correct answer to such speculations. It can trace the growth rate and some of its ramifications through the maze of daily activities in a modern metropolitan economy, but it cannot tell whether our rate, or any other, is best. The answer to that question depends upon your judgment, and the judgment of the others you live among. The question in the end is what we want, what kind of metropolitan life we care about, and how much we are prepared to pay to reach one goal as opposed to others. Growth and productivity are important measures for us to watch, but they do not come anywhere near to defining the totality of our lives, either as individuals or as a human settlement.

Buried in the 1930-42 income details of the three families of the scenario in Table III-A is an important message about how our economy functions during depressions. Michael, Sam, and Manuel's real incomes rose during the depression decade as did Annette's. Much of that increase came from the age grading of wages, but some of it, about ten percent of their total wages, came from increased productivity in their industries and from the relative decline in the prices of goods they purchased.

In short the iron law of demand and supply did not operate smoothly for labor during this sort of crisis. According to the old reasoning the wages of labor should have fallen in response to massive unemployment, and should have fallen so low that the unemployed could have been hired profitably. That did not happen. Employers endeavored to keep on their senior workers, workers defended their jobs with unions and family networks. Employers invested in new machinery to cut production costs. The end result of these retrenchments was more output per worker, not more workers. As a consequence unemployment lines remained long, and those who could hold on to their jobs slowly reaped the harvest of productivity.

Chronic unemployment, and periodic unemployment, thus appear to be salient conditions of our economy. Both have dominated the Boston scene since 1926. Those who are in the economy have more security than our free enterprise rhetoric suggests; and those who are out of the economy are far out indeed. The lessons of the Great Depression of the 1930's repeat themselves with each recession, and each time they surprise us. Imagine our governments and politicians rediscovering unemployment, as they all did during these past few years! If the end of unemployment be one of our goals, then these lessons of the past suggest that we must do more than tinker with taxes and subsidies for private employers. The Great Depression suggests that these remedies just provide more benefits for those inside the economy, and little for those waiting outside.

Next, examine the differences among the families. The Whites individually and jointly earn more than the Blacks or the Silvas. Again the cause of the difference is multiple. The Whites earn more than the Blacks because they are of the white race and opportunities for high wage jobs are more open to whites than blacks. The Silvas earn a little more than the Blacks for the same reason, but the gap between the two families is narrow.

The variations are not because the Whites are of Irish descent, and the Silvas are Portuguese and French-Canadian. Rather the Whites and the Blacks have an advantage over the Silvas because they work at the center of the metropolis where wages are the highest, and the Silvas work in the low-wage fringe.

Every metropolis in America has a geography of wages which resembles the Boston one. At the center where communications are easiest and most intense, finance and government flourish because they depend upon communications. So do the innovative industries, universities and hospitals, firms and institutions which deal in products that have not yet been standardized for production lines. All are firms that need a lot of highly skilled labor. The communications necessity reflects itself in the demand for labor, especially expensive labor, and this necessity gives the center the highest wages in the metropolitan region.

The process is a dynamic one in which firms

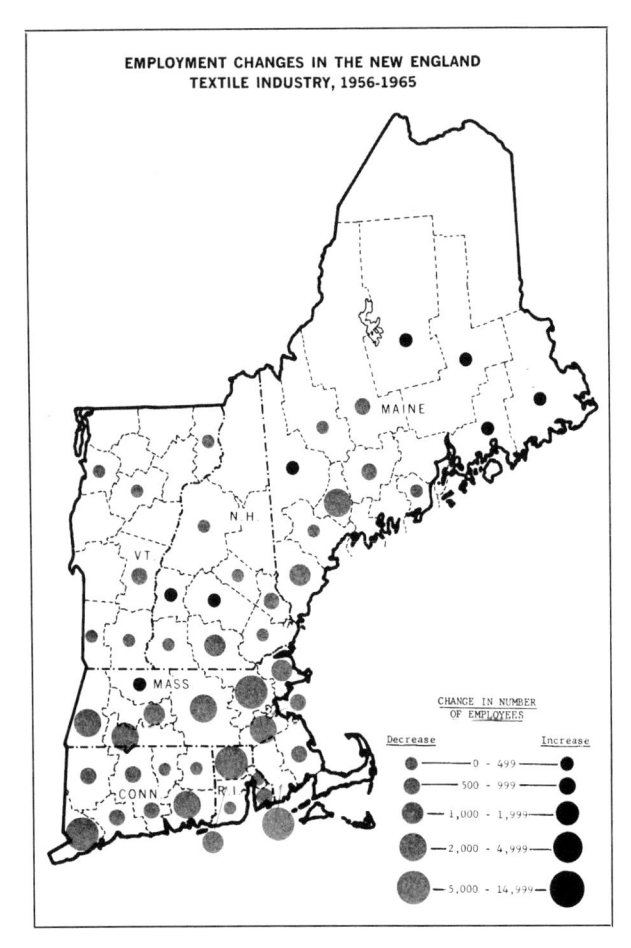

Fig. III-1
Employment Changes in the New England Textile Industry, 1956-1965

Source: *New England Business Review* (June 1967).

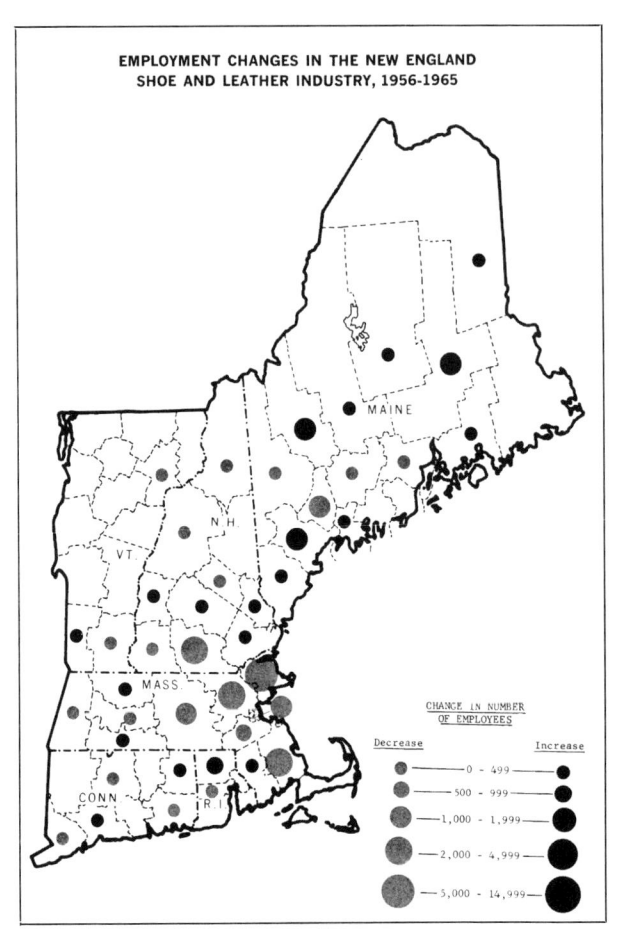

Fig. III-2
Employment Changes in the New England Shoe and Leather Industry, 1956-1965

Source: *New England Business Review* (June 1967).

quickly change locations in response to new opportunities. Some years ago the Federal Reserve Bank of Boston prepared maps of the shifting employment locations of two old production industries, textiles and shoes and leather, and one industry with a good deal of novelty in it, electrical machinery. The maps in Figures III-1, III-2, III-3 show changes in the decade 1956-65.

The industries with new products grew near the center, the old production industries sought the

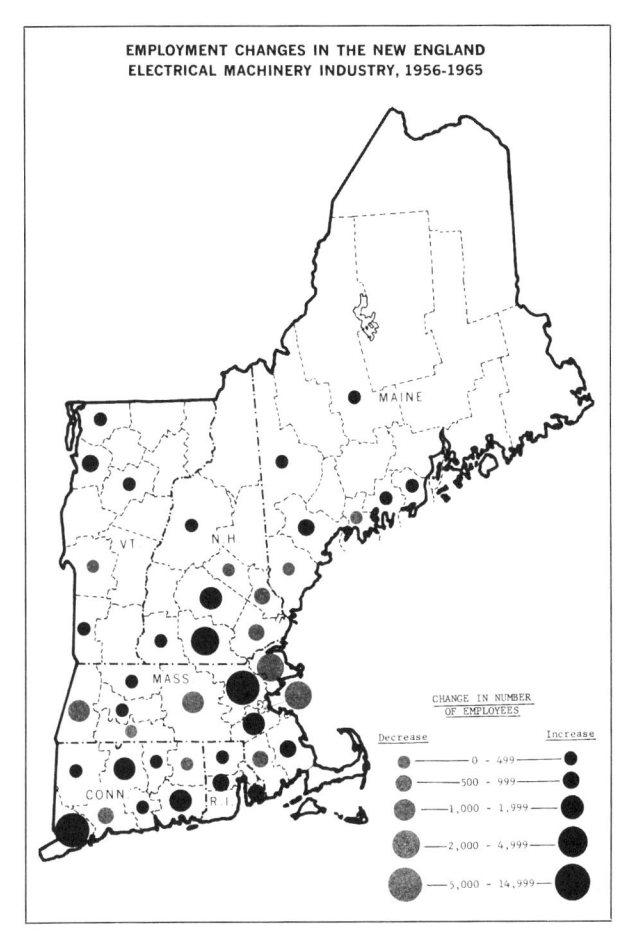

Fig. III-3
Employment Changes in the New England Electrical Machinery Industry, 1956-1965

Source: *New England Business Review* (June 1967).

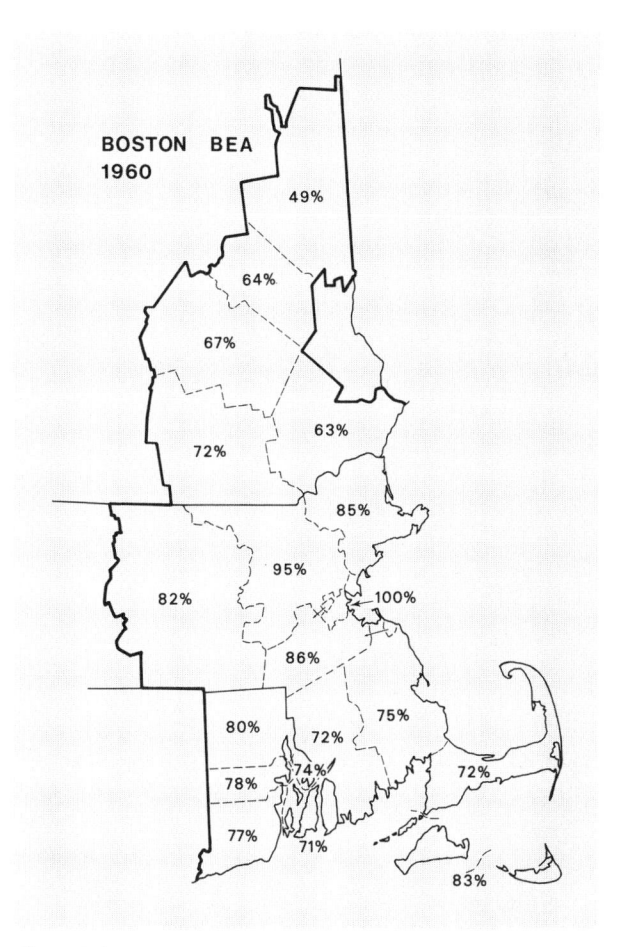

Fig. III-4
White Males, Average Yearly Wages, 1973, by Counties as Percentage of White Male Wages in Highest Wage County
(Measured in constant 1974 dollars at workplace address)

Note: Suffolk County average yearly wage equals $12,301; Boston BEA average yearly wage equals $9,349.

low wages of the Boston fringe, or left the region entirely.

A map of average wages for white males (Fig. III-4) summarizes the net effects of the many shifts in location which go on during any year in the metropolis. The wage levels of 1973 are given by county as a percentage of the county with the highest wages (in 1974 dollars)—Suffolk County, The Hub.

The effects of racial discrimination appear in a similar map (Fig. III-5) which plots black male wages. The peak wages for black males appear in Middlesex and Essex Counties, not in Suffolk. Perhaps the new electronics and other manufacturing establishments in these suburban areas offered more opportunity to blacks than the old food and clothing plants and service trades of central Boston.

The combination of racial difference and metropolitan wage geography explains almost all the differences in income among the three families in the scenario. After years of work, and after their children have grown, the Whites can reach the level of the single-family house and suburban life of our metropolis. The Blacks, working equally hard and long can never do so. Moreover, their low wages probably prevent them from paying rents sufficient to finance the expensive maintenance which the old wooden homes of inner Boston require. The Blacks, and families like them, must use up the inherited fixed capital of our metropolis.

The Silvas' lives are as limited as the Blacks, but I have speculated that by the use of the labor and capital of their parents—by Annette's mother taking care of the children while she works in the mills, and by the parents helping with the down payment on the two-family house—the Silvas can achieve homeownership. Again low income and low rents will threaten the maintenance of the working-class housing stock of their community— New Bedford.

None of these families could have achieved the living standard they did without the labor of the wives. As in the case of the men's earnings, geography, industry, and race explain the differences among the women. Maureen earns more than Malvina because she is white, but Malvina earns more than Annette because Annette is working at the Boston fringe. More significant than the distinctions among the women, is their difference from the men. Our sex-graded wage scales and limited openings for women to highly paid jobs restricts their earnings to about half that of their husbands. Figure III-6 is the same kind of metropolitan wage map showing white women's earnings. No separate map need be made for black women because their earnings are so close to those of their white sisters.

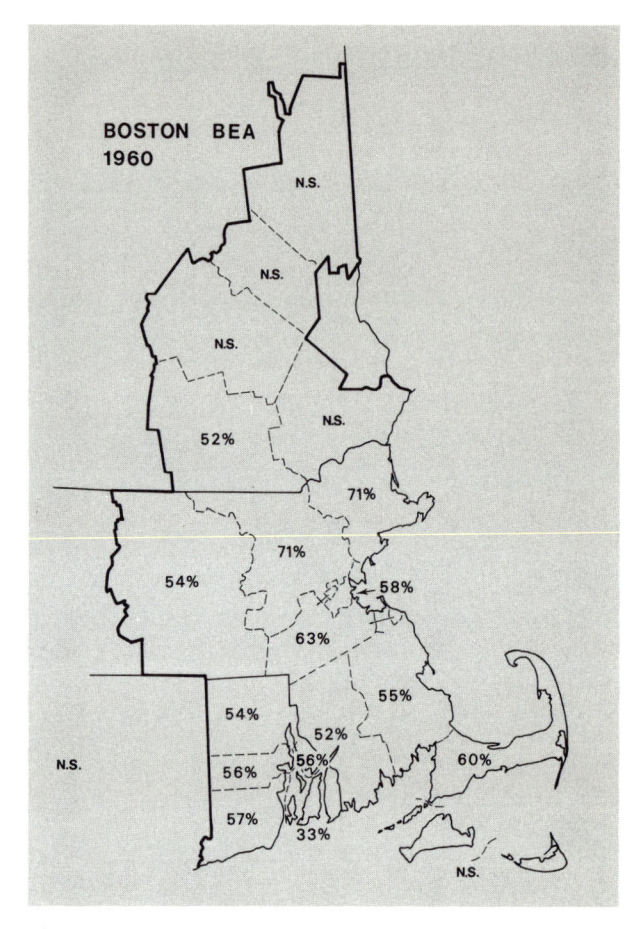

Fig. III-5
Black Males, Average Yearly Wages, 1973, by Counties as Percentage of White Male Wages in Highest Wage County
(Measured in constant 1974 dollars at workplace address)

Note: White males average yearly wage in Suffolk County equals $12,301; black males average yearly wage in Boston BEA equals $6,924.
N.S.: Black workforce too small for statistical reliability.

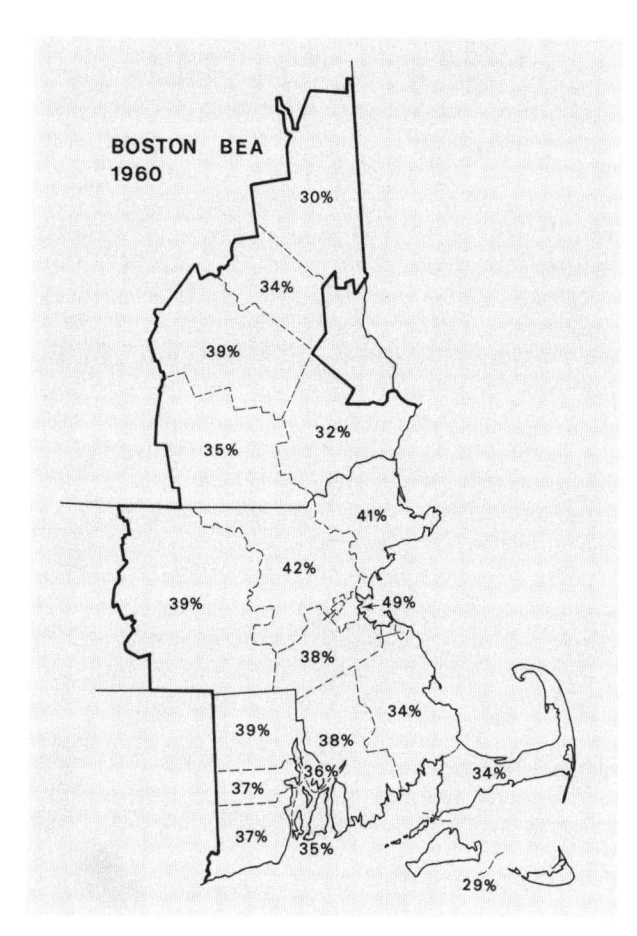

Fig. III-6
White Females, Average Yearly Wages, 1973, by Counties as Percentage of White Male Wages in Highest Wage County
(Measured in constant 1974 dollars at workplace address)

Note: White males average yearly wage in Suffolk County equals $12,301; white females average yearly wage in Boston BEA equals $4,497; black females average yearly wage in Boston BEA equals $4,414.

At issue is not the constraints and necessities of the economy, but the persistence of nineteenth-century family arrangements. In 1936 when the wives in our scenario contemplate leaving their husbands, our custom would have dictated that they take their children with them. Although the duty of the law is clear enough, women's experience in collecting alimony and child support from their former husbands suggests that this source is but an uncertain revenue. Thus, for the women and their children to separate from their husbands is to face a future of extreme poverty. Perhaps one of our Boston mottos is, "a hungry mother is a happy wife."

Even though the women's earnings are low, their families faced an economic crisis when they stopped working to stay at home to give birth and to raise children. In time the age-graded wage scale mitigated against this family loss. By 1940 the husbands are earning as much as the couple did together, fourteen years earlier, but the lower the family's income at first pregnancy the more severe the crisis.

Should the gap between men's and women's wages, and the differences in job opportunities be closed due to social and political pressure, families would find themselves pulled in several directions at once. Separation and divorce would become easier and less disastrous for wives. Family formation would also be easier since the new couples would be combining more or less equal earnings. As a result both the rate of divorce and the rate of marriage would rise among us, as they have since 1920.

The income crisis at pregnancy, and the consequences of the wife's staying at home would grow more severe since the relative loss of income would be larger as the wife's wages foregone approached the size of her husband's paychecks. This rising relative penalty might further encourage family limitation, and be an added force to recent trends in this direction. At the same time the lure of good pay might encourage women to keep on working. Part-time work would be especially sought after. Such an adjustment would continue the strong historic trend toward the increasing institutionalization of our children. If you are now unhappy with our schools, how are you going to like public daycare? The fate of our children (people, by the way, whom we have taken pains to put outside the economy) seems to be thus one of the most indeterminate and worrisome aspects of the past half-century family and economic trends.

One of the many strange aspects of our life together is the odd tasks to which we set the public parts of our economy. Over the years since 1920 the public sector of the economy, its debts, its purchases, and its employment, has become a substantial fraction of our economic activity. Currently the largest segment of the federal budget is devoted to protecting us against overseas threats—people like the Koreans, the Vietnamese, the Chinese, the Russians, and the Cubans—and it is also tied to servicing the debts incurred in past wars. Most of the balance of the federal budget, and a major share of state expenditures as well, is devoted to picking up the cast-offs of the private economy—old-age payments and unemployment benefits. Two additional large items, what we generally call welfare and education, are public tasks which assume what were formerly family duties. The former softens the blows of the breakup of poor families, the latter gives institutional care for all children. In our scenario the Whites paid 18.5% of their top earnings, the Blacks 15.9%, and the Silvas 15.5% for these public benefactions.

In discussing this public economy, however, we do not use as a test the goals of a family, the nurture of children and adults, neither do we ask the basic family question—are people better off for this program or that? Instead we reify the abstractions of the science of economics itself. Both President Carter and Governor Dukakis repeat over and over, as if they were saying something meaningful, the statements that the goals of our governments should be to restore a high economic growth rate, to end inflation, and to end unemployment. In the abstract all seem sensible enough goals to me, but they are empty statements. They have no meaning because they are never translated into the realities of everyday life. They are not translated either according to the numerical conventions of the men of science, or according to the metaphors of the men of letters. Without such translations one cannot judge how many missiles we would forego for day-care centers, or whether the possibilities of college scholarships should be set aside for a new airplane.

Especially bizarre is our absorption with taxation. The fixation grips politicians and citizens alike. By popular reasoning taxation is money lost. Tax money once out of one's private pocket and sent to a government becomes in its new location a different specie than private coin. It need not be accounted for like private money. Indeed government funds are something like the family cash jar which is set aside for parties and liquor. The total in the jar is of the utmost concern, but no accounting of the details of the expenditure is expected.

For example, our cities and towns have no uniform accounting system. More important they have no budget which records the impact upon their residents of the monies they spend. The same obscurantism prevails in the three states. Indeed, I am told that the accounts of the Commonwealth of Massachusetts have flourished into such a multiplicity that no one can even say with any certainty how many people the state has on its payroll on any given day.

The data we have been using in these lectures come from the federal government. They were the product of a relatively recent effort by economists who wanted to view the government not as just a fiscal body, but as an actor in the national and regional economies of the United States. The matter is serious. Unless we move beyond our obsession with taxation as a measure of good government, we will be foreclosed from deploying our public efforts to our greatest mutual benefit.

Let us begin an alternative kind of economic thinking. Let us attempt an exercise in which we apply our knowledge of family and community life in the Boston metropolis to the setting of some national and regional economic goals. Perhaps we can improve on the abstract statements of growth, employment, and monetary stability.

The review of the family consequences of average economic conditions here in Boston since 1920 immediately pinpoints a dominant quality of our life together: too many poor people live among us. More than half the families of Boston earned less than the Whites, the Blacks, and the Silvas.

To my view the growth in real incomes over the past fifty years, a gain of about two-and-a-half times, is an important accomplishment for the well-being of our human settlement. Yet the persistent relative poverty of so many of our fellow Bostonians is, and long has been, a scandal.

We parcel our incomes in much the same way we did in 1920. By so doing we create unnecessary private suffering in our families, and we exacerbate almost every problem of community life—our racial prejudices, our sexual prejudices, our housing and neighborhood maintenance, our environmental controls, our education, even our taxation.

Our income distribution not only perpetuates relative poverty among us and thereby degrades all manner of personal and community life, it also creates an obscene reward system for the most successful Bostonians.

The wealthy among us are twice rewarded by our customs. First, by the power of their roles as managers, employers, and leaders of our metropolis. As the governors of our institutions the rich direct our economy and have a disproportionate effect upon our culture, its politics, its journalism, its education, its arts, letters, and science.

The second reward, high personal income, adds to the first advantage by enabling the families of the wealthy to privatize our scarce resources. Their large houses, their cars, their yachts and airplanes consume indecent amounts of energy, they hold as family preserves many of our best seashores, marshes, meadows, and forests, and they control most of our cultural institutions and endeavors.

I do not mean by saying this that the wealthy are either more or less virtuous than the rest of us, only that our system of rewarding the powerful among us is wasteful and destructive to our community life. If we have in recent years learned to be concerned with the dangerous effects of extreme power imbalances in the family, should we not be equally concerned with such power imbalances in our metropolitan life?

Such logic leads immediately to the demand that we direct our economy so that it alters its income distribution. In short we should have an incomes goal for our economy. Here, as in the case of the rate of growth, economics cannot tell us how much redistribution we should seek; it is a matter for our experience and judgment.

Let us begin with a hypothetical example as a method of exploring together what is involved in setting an incomes policy. First, we will divide the personal incomes of United States residents into conventional groups. Then we will shift incomes about so that the personal incomes of Americans will rise in equal steps until the average person in the top income group earns only six times what the average person earns in the bottom group. In 1964 (the last year of a fairly long consistent time series) the range of average earnings of the groups was 25 to 1. What would happen if the range were reduced to 6 to 1?

Consider Table III-B and for the moment concentrate on the 1964 income distribution. On the left are the groupings of incomes into intervals which made practical sense in that year: the income categories of less than $2,999, $3,000 to $4,999, etc. Next is a list of the numbers of American families in each category: relatively small numbers at the bottom and the top, a large middle cluster.

To make these figures meaningful in today's terms the average income for each group was calculated and then inflated to an income equivalent to today's wages and prices. Note that the average income for all American families in 1964 when translated into 1974 dollars stood at $13,388. One powerful argument for income redistribution rests on the observation that more than half the families earn less than this average income. That is, the *median* income lies below the average because the high incomes at the top pull the average up. This effect can be seen in the table. The lowest three income groups earn on the average $9,464 or less. These same groups totalled 51.2% of all the families (the sum of the percentages of the families in the bottom three groups).

The special quality of our income distribution is thus its skewed allocation of total income. The top two groups, 9.9% of all American families, got 28.1% of the income; the bottom two groups, 27.9% of the families, got 9.8% of the income.

Some of this skewed distribution was caused by our age-graded wage scales. That is young people contribute disproportionately to the low-income

TABLE III-B
Distribution of Aggregate Personal Income By Families, United States 1935/36, 1964 (All income before taxes)

1935/36

Income Category $	No. Families (thousands)	Group Av. Income 1974 $	Group % Total Income	% Total Families
< 999	11,624	2,129	12.5	38.2
1,000-1,999	10,894	5,268	29.0	35.2
2,000-2,999	4,595	8,826	20.5	15.1
3,000-4,999	2,191	13,364	14.8	7.2
5,000-7,499	548	22,026	6.1	1.8
7,500+	548	61,738	17.1	1.8
	30,400			

NOTE: Average Family Income $6,507.

1964

< 2,999	5,590	2,741	2.4	11.7
3,000-4,999	7,740	6,104	7.4	16.2
5,000-7,499	11,133	9,464	16.5	23.3
7,500-14,999	18,682	15,587	45.6	39.1
15,000-24,999	3,536	27,249	15.2	7.4
25,000+	1,194	68,990	12.9	2.5
	47,875			

NOTE: Average Family Income $13,388.

1964 Hypothetical Redistribution

Income Levels				
X	5,590	4,145	3.6	11.7
2X	7,740	8,289	10.0	16.2
3X	11,133	12,434	21.7	23.3
4X	18,682	16,579	48.5	39.1
5X	3,536	20,723	11.5	7.4
6X	1,194	24,879	4.7	2.5
	47,875			

NOTE: Average Family Income $13,388.

SOURCE: *Historical Statistics of the U.S.*, vol. 1, Tables G269-296.

group, but the age distribution of the population does not mirror the income distribution, and many wage-earners of the poor families are middle-aged and old.

In the hypothetical exercise it seems best to disturb society as little as possible. Since our custom is to rank families hierarchically, to have a few at the top, many in the middle, and large contingent at the bottom, let us leave these feelings untouched. We seem to like to feel superior to the Joneses; it seems to us a proper way for human beings to live together. The hypothetical problem thus becomes a question of redistributing income in such a way that the average income of the wealthiest group is six times that of the poorest group, leaving the social hierarchy as it stands. In the column which shows the distribution of families among the groups there is therefore no change between the actuality of 1964 and the pretended new situation. Also because we are dividing a fixed pie, not changing the total amount of income, the average size of the piece, the average income per family, also does not change.

The six-to-one rule accomplishes its redistribution in two ways. First, notice it moved money from the top two groups to the four below them. The percentage share of total income rose from 2.4 to 3.6 for the bottom group, from 7.4 to 10.0 for the next, from 16.5 to 21.7 for the next, and 45.6 to 48.5 for the next. If the bottom two groups are the poor, and the top two groups the rich, and the two center groups the middle class, then in this hypothetical exercise we added 8.1% to the middle class's share, and we gave the poor only 3.8% more. It has the true ring of American reform doesn't it?

I leave to your judgment whether such a change would be desirable. You must also form an opinion about whether such a change would be ambitious, and therefore cost much social and political effort, or whether such a change is modest, and therefore relatively easy to accomplish. The sums involved are not beyond the ordinary business of the federal government. Before the hypothetical change the top groups earned 179.4 billion dollars, after the exercise they were left with 102.9 billion. We took 76.5 billion dollars from them for our redistribution scheme. Such a sum is equal to the the pre-Vietnam United States Defense Department budget for 1964, according to the Bureau of the Census' *Statistical Abstract: 1971.*

We did more than move money from the top to the lower groups, we also steepened the steps of the hierarchy. By postulating formal steps, by insisting that each group receive one equal increment more than its predecessor on the list, the exercise spread out the groupings so that they became farther apart in their income averages. In 1964 the steps, from the bottom upward, were (in 1974 dollars) $2,741, $6,104, $9,464, and $15,587; they became $4,000, $8,000, $12,000, and $16,000. The intervals among the bottom three grew larger, the interval between the third and fourth smaller.

These shifts in average income among the groups remind us that there are three issues which must be kept in mind simultaneously when thinking about income policies. First, what is a desirable range of incomes? second, what should the steps be in the hierarchy? third, how many people ought to be in each step? Language and method for thinking about these problems are provided by Lester Thurow in a sophisticated analysis of the nature and causes of the present distribution of income and wealth, *Generating Inequality: Mechanisms of Distribution in the U.S. Economy.*

The answers to these questions, once again, are not to be found in the science of economics, they lie in your judgment of the nature of our society and your view about what its goals should be.

To conclude, and to prepare you for the next lecture's speculations about the alternatives open to the Boston metropolitan economy, let me call your attention to a small, but significant, comparison between the 1935/6 income distribution and the 1964 one. In the earlier years the top two income groups consisted of 3.6% of all American families and together they earned 23.3% of all the nation's income. In 1964 the top two groups consisted of 9.9% of all American families, and they earned 28.1%. Given the increase in their numbers the per-family income share has declined markedly since 1935/6.

In the downtown clubs, in the legislative halls, on academic platforms, in books and magazines we have all been telling each other that the cause of this decline of great fortunes was the federal income tax and the ferocity of Franklin Delano Roosevelt and his successors. Hogwash, all of it.

All our calculations in this lecture have been based on reports of income *before* taxes.

The change at the top was not the product of taxes but of shifts in the rewards system of our mixed private and public economy. Professionals, managers, and bureaucrats have been multiplying since 1935. Their institutions, corporations, universities, hospitals, and government offices, have also been multiplying. Investment of capital has ceased to be the province of a few individuals of great wealth and instead has become the business of bankers, pension and investment fund managers, insurance executives, and corporate officers. These men and their assistants and technicians have expanded the numbers in the top ranks, the $27-68,000 groups, but few earn great fortunes. Perhaps you have noticed that Cape Cod and the Islands are growing with luxury summer homes, and in the harbors there is a shortage of berths for small boats. These resorts are not growing with great landed estates, and the steam yacht has given way to the racing sloop.

Such income redistribution as did take place in the United States came as the consequence of shifts in the institutional arrangements of our economy: unions and the multiplication of professional and managerial roles.

With our sights fixed upon taxes we do not look for, or notice such changes. Glued to the tax forms we cannot see that our economy changes in many ways, and therefore we fail to think that there are as many ways to improve it.

If one were of a conspiratorial turn of mind, one would surely believe that the federal income tax was invented by a reactionary capitalist president bent on keeping us all ignorant of the working of our economy and its governments. That president's name was Woodrow Wilson.

IV.

A Humane Economy

The family, though a durable human grouping which reproduces itself over and over in history despite wars, famines, and racial extermination, is a naked institution. It possesses few barriers save a front door, and little capital to protect it from disaster.

In the last lecture we translated some aggregate statistics of the present and past wages of the economy into scenarios which suggested the constraints and achievements of commonplace lives in Boston since 1920. All the boundaries of family life lay outside the power of a single ordinary citizen's ability to transform them. Earnings in Boston, like those elsewhere in the United States, have been, and are, determined by long-standing customs of paying differing amounts, and offering different jobs to men than to women, to white men as opposed to black men, to the early middle-aged, as opposed to the young and the old. None of these customs find much, if any justification, in the needs of an active economy for efficiency. Rather they are our customs.

The only strongly economic basis for the differences among the earnings of Boston families stemmed from the advantages of location. Firms near the center of the metropolis seek more skilled labor and pay higher wages than those at the fringe. This differential has its origin in the more intense communications which are possible at the center of a metropolis as opposed to what can be achieved at the outer fringe. The geographic differential in wages, however, has declined since the 1920's, so that while in 1926 (Fig. IV-1) northern Carroll County, New Hampshire, had a per capita income which was but one third that of Norfolk County, Massachusetts, by 1970 (Fig. IV-2) the income differential had declined to a level where Carroll County residents earned two thirds what Norfolk County residents did. The automobile by dispersing jobs outward from the center, and by lengthening commuting lines has softened the penalties of distance and has created a more geographically even economy.

No substantial change, however, took place in the distribution of income among the families of Boston without regard to their location. The poor, the middle classes, and the rich still exist in about

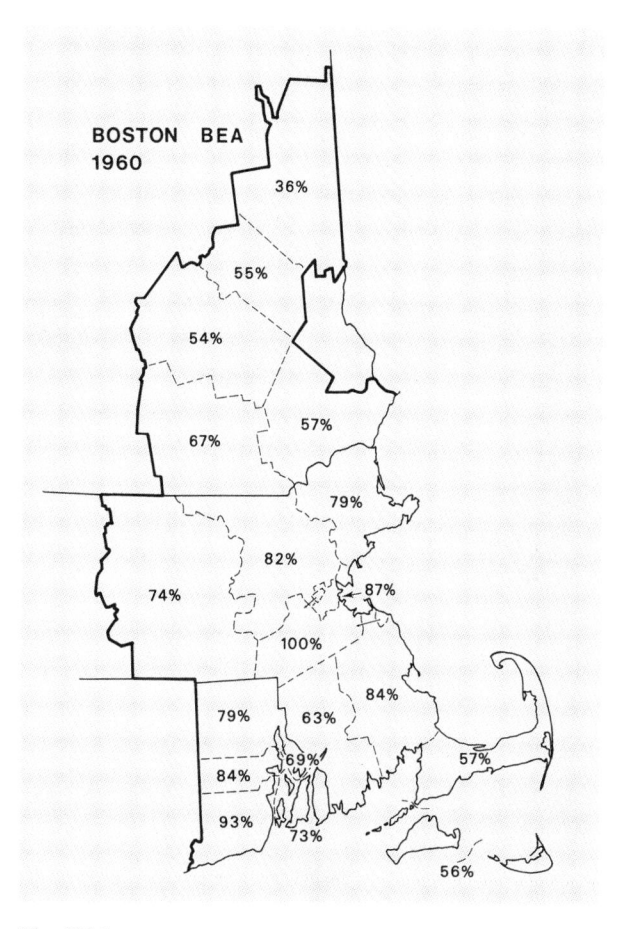

Fig. IV-1
Per Capita Income by Percent of Wealthiest County, 1926
(Measured in constant 1974 dollars at residence address)

Note: Per capita income for Norfolk County equals $3,824.

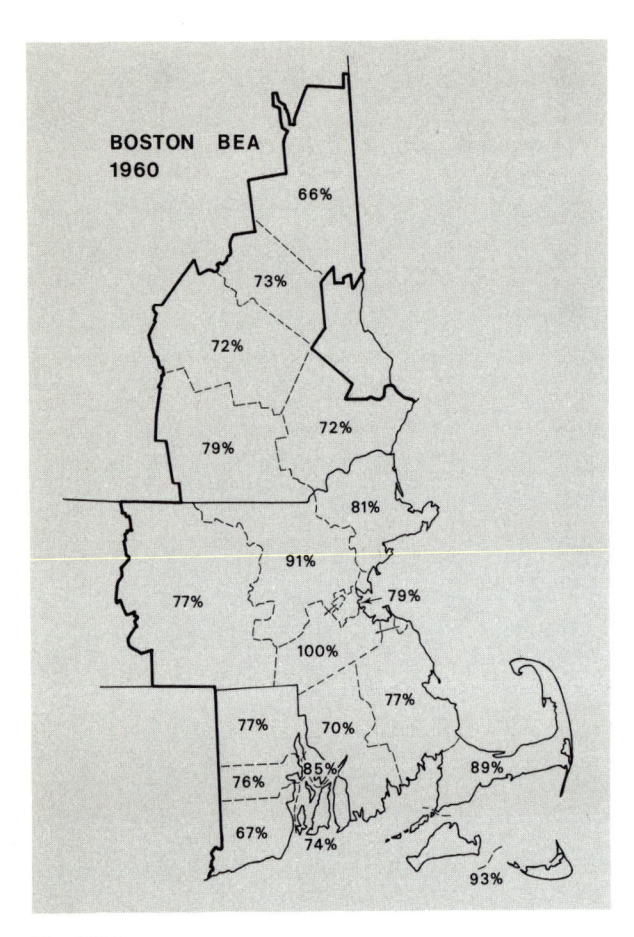

Fig. IV-2
Per Capita Income by Percent of Wealthiest County, 1970
(Measured in constant 1974 dollars at residence address)

Note: Per capita income for Norfolk County equals $6,566.

the same proportions today as they did in the depths of the Great Depression. This stability persisted in the face of a rapid and universal rise in the real incomes of Bostonians, an increase of about two-and-a-half times since 1920. The consequence has been an obdurate social hierarchy which rewards some excessively, and holds many in relative poverty.

The extreme nature of the rewards of our economy exacerbates about every activity we identify as a problem today: education, childcare, crime, housing, transportation, racial and sexual prejudice, the natural environment.

The obstinate economic fact of Boston and American life thus centers around our unwillingness as a society to set income goals for our economy. In discussing what the setting of such goals would involve we noted that some income redistribution had taken place among those in the top bracket. This redistribution was not the consequence of taxation, as is popularly believed, but emerged from shifts in the nature of wealth and the manner of doing business. Changes in the way we transact our business, private and public, have reduced the numbers of people with great fortunes, and have multiplied the number of highly-paid professionals and managers. This observation of past trends led to the suggestion that if we would think in more various terms than just taxation we might be able to set and attain goals for our economy which would make Boston, and the United States, a more humane, more life-supporting, place to live.

That lead gained from watching the income figures will be the subject for this lecture. What should we think about, if we wished to mitigate the severity of our economic environment?

The first step, and the precondition to all others, must be to account to each other more fully and accurately what we in fact do. We noted last time the vagueness of our public expenditures, an obscurity maintained in the face of the growing importance of public activities in our economy. Elsewhere I have spoken of the necessity for improvement of reports on private economic activity. I will not repeat the call. It should be sufficient to note that most of the economic statistics we have been using in these lectures are of recent origin. They are the result of much private and public research undertaken with the goal of making the economy translatable into meaningful terms which could test whether public or private economic activities had a benign or destructive effect on regional and national life. Thanks to this labor, the work of the past half-century, we can easily maintain public accounts which tell what public and private actions do to wages, employment, income, investment, local and export businesses. Today we lack only the willingness to take collective responsibility for our economic roles.

There are historical reasons why a statistic which measures some aspects of the daily price of money, the Dow Jones Average of the New York Stock Exchange, is broadcast to us daily while what we need to know about trends in wages, employment, food, land, and housing are given in quarterly or monthly press releases of little action value. Again there are historical reasons why we all talk about taxes, but have no measure of the consequences of the government activities at our command. Yet, if we are to become serious about making our economic life more humane, we must seize the capabilities of our modern knowledge and technique.

Let us talk about the past and present conditions of the Boston economy in terms which deal with the constraints and possibilities of our economy. At all times we must watch both our position in the nation, and our local situation: it is the blending of these two characteristics which governs our private wages and profits, and limits our public undertakings.

Boston is a resource-poor region: water, air, trees, sand, gravel and stones are all the natural resources that abound. The metropolis is close to the populous urbanized northeast markets, but it is on the fringe, and it is far indeed from steel, copper, petroleum, corn and wheat. Robert Eisenmenger's book, *The Dynamics of Growth in the New England Economy*, is devoted to an analysis of how such a region functions. To render his careful calculations in a sentence: such a region trades its labor for resources.

Boston prospers, or languishes, according to the outcomes of its sales of labor-intensive products and services. A complicated machine like a computer, or a complicated service like a hospital, both of which use relatively few materials and much labor, are ideal products for such a place. So too are all manner of less glamorous undertakings like the manufacture of special tools, the custom building of unusual ships, the proffer of business and investment services, the keeping of schools, or the running of restaurants for tourists.

In terms of its history, Boston's past is a story of the early introduction of the machines of industrialization followed by a steady loss of this initial advantage as other parts of the nation developed. The advantage melted away in three directions. The westward settlement of the continent carried customers farther and farther from us. The location of modern production near the sources of coal, iron, petroleum, and foodstuffs put our companies at a disadvantage whenever they undertook to sell commonplace items beyond New England. The abundance of cheap labor elsewhere in the nation, especially in the south and midwest, drew labor intensive mass product industries like furniture, shoes, garments, and textiles to these locations.

These are the familiar ingredients of the standard narrative of the decline of Boston. Mr. Eisenmenger's book is a careful working out of the wage implications of this history. Today ours is a low-wage region. For most occupations, from janitor to plant manager, wage levels are about ten percent below the national average, and they are likely to remain at such a discount because we must import our raw materials and sell at a long distance.

This wage differential is not a statistic known only to technicians, but is common knowledge among us. For decades people have been leaving Boston seeking an easier economic life in other parts of the nation. For example, according to the United States Department of Commerce, of those working in the Boston BEA during 1960, and who were subsequently continuously covered by Social Security, 160,000 people left the region to work elsewhere. In their new homes these outmigrants were earning during the year 1970 $1,500 more per year than those who chose to stay in Boston. Most of these migrants went to New York, Ohio, Illinois, Texas, and California. All places with important economic advantages we do not have.

The fact of low wages and the necessity to concentrate on labor-intensive production does not, however, prevent us from making ourselves more comfortable. It does put a premium on doing what we do well, and upon arranging our economy so that it is as supportive of a labor-intensive society as possible. In economic terms our principal asset is human capital and therefore it is important that we manage it well. Nor are we as isolated in this condition as we once were. As natural resources grow more and more expensive the rest of the nation will soon join us in this predicament.

We think of Boston as an old place, a place where tradition and the past endure. Not so for our economy. The essence of our situation is change—unpredictable change. No specialty can be secure because some natural resource, like rich farm land, or deep seams of coal, perpetuate it. Rather we must always be seeking new markets, new ways of doing things, new fashions, new specialties. Here, with the economy, we meet at a faster pace, the same indeterminacy that we met in the history of the family. Both are changeful things and we cannot know today what will be the best arrangement for the future. We must learn to live with uncertainty, with the repeated failure of seemingly promising new starts, and with the repeated failure of ossified businesses, government programs, and public and private institutions.

The largest event of our recent economic history, the collapse of the century-old textile industry, mirrors our present situation. Textiles are a labor-intensive industry whose early mechanization brought great wealth to the Boston region. First the abandonment of farms in New England, and then the importation of immigrants from Europe and Canada kept wages here low enough for the industry to prosper. Beginning in 1890 the modernization of agriculture in the southeast freed its labor for millwork and Boston's early advantage melted away. Only the military orders of World War I and World War II halted the decline. The 1930 census showed that after four years of textile depression the mills in Massachusetts, Rhode Island, and New Hampshire still employed 264,000 workers. By 1970, the census showed that their number had dropped to 61,000. A net loss of 203,000 jobs! Ten percent of the three states' 1930 labor force, 7% of their 1970 labor force.

Think for a moment of the impact of such a change. Think not only of the workers themselves, but also of their families, the merchants and suppliers and related industries which depended on them. This shift alone could have accounted for continuous depression and high unemployment in the region from 1926 on. Since other old industries also lost ground for similar reasons chronic unemployment stalked the region in all years except during the wars. Given this experience no one can say today that our unemployment insurance and welfare programs have made such inevitable transitions a humane process among us here in Boston.

More satisfactory relief, relief in the form of good jobs, came from the subsequent development of new industries and new lines of work to replace the textile losses. The source of this relief was unexpected—no one saw it coming until perhaps World War II or later. The relief was also not the result of unfettered private enterprise, nor was it the result of farsighted government planning and investment. Rather it was the surprising outcome of both public and private activity.

The new industries, high technology industries, like electronics, emerged from two public sources. The ideas and the trained personnel came from the universities of the region, especially from M.I.T. Now universities are themselves very much mixed enterprises. They derive support from fees and private gifts, but they also are the beneficiaries of continuous public subsidy—the exemption from local, state, and federal taxation. Second, during World War II and the Cold War years that followed, the federal government poured millions of dollars into applied and basic scientific research. Finally, federal purchases of military supplies created a profitable market for scientists and businessmen who undertook to apply the new science. The military orders gave capital and experience to infant firms which in time expanded outwards to civilian markets in business machines, communications and computer equipment, and all manner of goods and services which are appropriate to our electronics age.

The changeover to high-technology, labor-intensive industries, an event which now looks so logical and inevitable, was quite unforeseen during the long dark years of the textile depression which ground relentlessly on from 1926 to 1942. You will look in vain in the studies of the twenties and thirties for predictions of relief from such a source. Prof. Charles Artman in his chapter in the 1933 *New England's Prospect* does try to stem the contemporary mood of pessimism by calling his readers' attention to the large electrical machinery industry which then existed in New England. But this industry was not then, as it is now, a big user of university-based science, nor a large employer of university-trained scientists.

For example, the Raytheon Corporation is a newcomer. Now a firm with 25 plants and 40,000 employees in New England, it was founded prior to World War II by an M.I.T. physicist, Dr. Vannevar Bush, with a very modest horizon: it began by making a better thermostat, reports Harold Latham, in a 1964 issue of the *Industrial Development and Manufacturers Record*. Without the nation's continuing wars and armaments the reorganization of the Boston economy would have been a much longer and more painful process.

There is an ugly repetition of history in all of this. Our first industrial prosperity rested upon slaves and cotton, our second on war and armaments.

I reason from this history that our economic future will continue to be unpredictable, and that the next successful cluster of industries will also be a surprise to us. At present the public support of universities seems a wise investment but it may not always be so. Universities are human institutions and like all such they have a tendency to ossify, as they did during the eighteenth century. There is no reason to believe that we may not some day in the future be creating new institutions for research and the development of useful knowledge.

Since the size and complexity of a modern metropolitan region requires more and more public activity to maintain it as a safe and pleasant place for human life, we must learn to develop balance sheets for public undertakings as well as private ones. We can have a much more humane economy if we will be more active and experimental in our public undertakings, but a consequence of such ambition will inevitably be a high failure rate. Closing public institutions and programs must become a routine among us, just as bankruptcy is in private business.

To give one example which has been at the forefront of everyone's attention in recent years: the Boston School Department is a large, costly, and significant institution in our metropolis. It has the responsibility for training 70,000 children each year. If it does this task well our human resources are improved for future years, and our expenditures are a good investment. If it does badly the consequences are as costly to us all as the plundering of the Penn Central Railroad. Surely both the children of Boston and their future contribution to our economy would now be better off if three years ago that calcified institution, the Boston School Department, had been closed and a fresh start made with a new institutional design.

In sum, given the exposed position of a labor-intensive region, and given our history of ceaseless change, a humane economy would be one which allowed that change, but also one which cushioned the family and community from the inevitable hardships that closings always bring.

You all know what is at issue in the protection of employees from the failure of their firms and institutions. The subject has occupied American social reform since 1900. Pensions must be vested and made safe and honest so that employees can move freely from one employer to the next without losing accumulated contributions. At present millions of public and private employees lack this minimal protection.

Unemployment insurance needs to be more closely tied to job finding, retraining, and moving assistance so that families do not become trapped in dead mill towns, or inner-city slums. Especially the job has to precede the training, so that the future worker can see the goal and not be faced with the all-too-common experience of today's programs in which people are trained for jobs which do not exist.

Finally, if all else fails, public employment at decent living wages has to be available for those who cannot be placed in regular work. To keep hands

TABLE IV-A

1930: Tri-state Area, Persons 10 Years Old and Over Engaged in Gainful Occupations, by Industry

	THREE STATES		DIFFERENCE FROM UNITED STATES	
	Males	Females	Males	Females
Civilian Labor Force As % Population 10+	75.8	29.1	-0.4	+7.0
Industry Group:				
Agriculture, Forestry, Fishing	5.8	0.6	-20.0	-7.9
Manufacturing	41.0	40.6	+16.4	+18.5
Mining	0.2	<0.1	-2.8	-0.1
Construction	8.9	0.4	+2.3	+0.1
Wholesale and Retail	15.0	11.1	+2.4	-1.1
Finance, Real Estate, and Insurance	2.9	3.7	+0.2	0
Trans., Communications, Pub. Utilities	9.8	3.4	-0.7	-0.8
Services	10.5	37.1	+1.8	-8.5
Public Adminis.	3.4	1.0	+1.0	-0.1
Not Specified	2.5	2.1	-0.4	-0.1
	100.0	100.0		

SOURCE: *U.S. Census:* 1930, vol. 3, Table 56, State Table 10.

idle on unemployment insurance or welfare is surely the most costly waste of our money and human capital which could be devised. As a society we need each other's labor, and as individuals we need a decent job at a living wage.

Such measures, extensions only of reform underway for the past century, would do a great deal towards redistributing income in favor of the low-wage families of the region and the nation. They would reduce the incidence of poverty among the old, the unemployed, and the underemployed. Finally, a living wage for public employment would, in effect, establish a minimum wage for all workers. The tax costs of these measures would be substantially offset by the economic stimulus of the greater spending power of the beneficiaries.

But to limit our public efforts to such a program is to fall short of a humane metropolitan economy. To stop at these goals is to turn all of our metropolis into a safer Framingham. It is to enact the standard European social democratic platform. Good as a beginning, but I think we have the right to hope we can do better.

TABLE IV-B

1970: Tri-state Area, Experienced Civilian Labor Force 16 Years and Older by Industry

	THREE STATES		DIFFERENCE FROM UNITED STATES	
	Males	*Females*	*Males*	*Females*
Civilian Labor Force As % Population 16+	75.4	44.8	+2.1	+3.8
Industry Group:				
Agric., Forestry, Fishing	1.5	0.4	-3.8	-0.7
Manufacturing	33.5	26.7	+3.8	+6.6
Mining	0.1	<0.1	-1.1	-0.2
Construction	9.3	-0.7	-0.2	-0.2
Wholesale and Retail	19.4	20.4	+0.5	-1.6
Finance, Real Estate, and Insurance	4.2	6.9	+0.2	+0.4
Trans. Communications, Pub. Utilities	6.8	3.4	-1.7	-0.4
Services	18.8	37.9	+2.0	-2.9
Public Adminis.	6.3	3.3	+0.2	-1.0
Not Specified	<0.1	0.2	-	-
	99.9	99.9		

SOURCE: *U.S. Census: 1970,* Table 235; State Tables 20, 183.

So far we have been considering our history in terms of the pains and problems of continuing readjustment. Suppose, instead of viewing our history in these terms, we gave our attention to the general trends which made our time easier and more prosperous than what preceded it. In this way we might find not just problems of transition, but also some new opportunities. The economist's grouping of employment into clusters according to general product lines, or according to services rendered, what is called an industrial grouping, will suit our purposes.

At the top of Tables IV-A and IV-B the percentage of workers in the total population shows what has been happening to wage labor since 1930. The major change has been the increasing commitment of women to paid labor and the concomitant substitution of mothers for boys in the economy. There is a slight decline in the proportion of the male population employed, even though the base of measurement was changed from all males 10 years and older to all males 16 years and older. The boys have been held out of the economy to attend school. On the female side the overall trend is in the opposite direction. The proportion of women increased markedly, it about doubled for the United States and was up 15% for our tri-state area. The three states show a gain which is less than the nation's because we had already by 1930 been in the habit of using large numbers of women in wage work.

The difference between the three-state area and the nation, as well as the 1930-1970 trends show again the situation of Boston as being in the forefront of national development. We should run tours for out-of-state residents not just to show people the remains of an old past, as we do now, but should introduce contemporary tours to let them see the future which is coming toward them.

Moving down the list of industrial groups, the agriculture category records our early and thorough loss of that specialty. Some economists think that the recent national trends towards higher food prices will in time create opportunities for agriculture in Boston once more.

Manufacturing in 1930 shows our industrialization headstart; the region was way ahead of the nation in employment of both men and women in these industries. Our 40-year direction, however, is just the reverse of the nation's. We lost in our proportions of males and females in manufacturing while the nation showed gains. This is the notorious statistic of New England's decline. More thoughtful and optimistic students, however, see in this decline in Boston the harbinger of a better future. These thinkers reason that mechanization means more and more products with less and less workers and that the labor freed from factories can move to more direct person-to-person activities in trade, finance, education, health, business, and government services. This school heralds a new service economy, something richer, easier, and more humane than the arduous machine-tending of the nineteenth century.

Mining in Boston during the twentieth century is chiefly the romance of the sand and gravel pit. The construction employment figures reflect a low-growth region. Skipping to transportation, communications, and public utilities we observe that the low percentage of workers in the three states as compared to the nation comes from our small geographical area and is also a consequence of an advanced economy which is not heavily engaged in moving raw materials.

The categories of regional growth and specialization lie in wholesale and retail trade, finance, real estate and insurance, and services. Our public administration employment hovers at the national average. You should be aware that the census definition of "public administration" and "public service" understates public employment because the census scatters government employees by function, sending the postmen to transport and communications, the school teachers to services, etc. Nevertheless the average level of public administration employees for the three states should quiet the fears of those among you who think that Boston is a region burdened with a special weight of time-serving civil servants.

The rise of the marketing, finance, service and government sectors of our economy should be taken as a sign of new opportunities and new problems. This grouping contains within it many export activities which generate regional wealth to trade for fuel and food. Boston sells higher education, health, and business services to nationwide markets, just as it formerly sold cloth and shovels. The shift also has its worrisome side. Many services are low-paying jobs—retailing, restaurants, and many levels of health care, pay their employees as relatively badly as the old mills did. Prof. Bennett Harrison, in his report on *The Economic Development of Massachusetts,* is one of those who are concerned that the increase in service jobs may be a sign of a depressed economy, not evidence of a new prosperity.

In preparing for these lectures I calculated for 1970 the relationship between per-capita income in each of the 20 counties and their level of earnings in three industrial groupings. The questions were: was a concentration on manufacturing associated with wealthy counties? or did high levels of services or state and local government employment go with prosperous counties? High per-capita personal income for county residents did not go with manufacturing (-.385), nor did it go with state and local government employment (-.192). Conversely, service employment was strongly and positively correlated with high per-capita income (+.568).

These correlations support the optimists in the United States Department of Commerce who see a prosperous future for the region in concentration on services. Yet Prof. Harrison is surely right to call our attention to the many low-wage jobs in this industry group. As we learned from looking at the income distributions in the last lecture, we are in 1970 treating many of our fellow citizens as badly with services as we did years ago with textile mills.

The recent growth of services, finance, marketing, and government gives an important clue to how we might manage our economy more humanely. Their increase suggests that with high technology, production makes many things cheaply, and that a new source of profit lies in marketing and servicing, areas beyond the competition of mechanized production.

Think for a moment how the signs have changed along the highway. Joe's Diner has become Macdonald's; Jim's Garage has become the Sears and Roebuck, or Goodyear Tire, service center. Discount houses have squeezed out small stores, first to market major appliances, then a whole range of commonplace items. Packaging and advertisement absorb greater and greater shares of the cost of most of the products you buy. In human services the trends have been similar. Larger and larger organizations, both bigger and more complicated hospitals and bigger and more complicated schools; have replaced their smaller and simpler 1920 counterparts. The new office towers of downtown Boston, and the suburban office parks tell the same story of larger corporate organizations replacing older, smaller forms.

As an urban historian I read these visible signs as the complement to the changes in the table of industrial employment groupings. The large automobile metropolis has offered new opportunities for national and regional marketing, and corporate enterprise has moved in to organize these opportunities and to capture the new profits. Where formerly the department store and the downtown landlord pocketed the profit of our tight clustering into a central city, now the national franchise, the shopping center, and the corporate retail and service outlet picks up the wealth we create by living in our new dispersed form. This is the new wealth we can tap for improving our economic life.

What are today's complaints about the economy? Too many wages are too low, and too many of the commonplace goods that go into our basic standard of living cost too much. We can meet these complaints in two ways: either by helping those who are paid little to receive more, or by reducing the price of commonplace goods like housing, food, transportation, clothing, basic appliances, education, and health care. Since monopoly profits prevail in all these lines, as the corporate entrance into them testifies, public intervention could capture these profits and use them either for raising wages or cutting prices.

All such interventions presuppose a good regional public and private accounting system, since each product and service has its own special character. General attacks like tax breaks and wage controls are too gross, too vague, and are therefore not likely to be helpful. The floundering of our national economic policy during the past four years makes this point clear enough.

Let us look at a few commonplace products and services with an eye to imagining appropriate public interventions.

Consider your food costs. The big marketing spread in food is not at the supermarket level, it lies between the farmer and the supermarket. Therefore state and federal intervention must take the form of altering current wholesale market practices, alterations which should be aimed at either raising the wages of farm workers or lowering consumer prices. My preference would be to aim for the former.

Or, think of our housing problems. Two issues leap forward—the cost of new houses and the maintenance of old ones. For the former a state land bank which purchased and sold land for development could either lower land costs for new construction or capture for the public the land profit which comes from our urban clustering. For old homes the purchase of cheap, honest, and appropriate repair services is the current problem. An answer might lie in the state creation of a few model corporations which organized and supervised the small craftsmen who rendered these services.

Education reveals opposite needs. On the one hand we have in the region a number of very unsuccessful large public systems and a number of successful private schools. The use of public vouchers for students and families trapped in failing school systems might give them an important benefit at reduced cost. On the other hand privately-managed trade schools have been taking their students' money for years without teaching them much. In this field new publicly-operated institutions seem indicated.

In short for each important product and service in our economy there is a somewhat unique set of circumstances. The remedies, therefore, must fit each case. Some interventions can only be undertaken at the federal level, as in many aspects of power, transport, food, and energy. Some can be primarily state and local measures, as in housing, education, health. I repeat once again, we cannot enjoy the benefits of such specific interventions unless we have an adequate regional and national accounting system, and unless we are willing to close out our failures.

Public interventions can and should be as various as the problems to be addressed. Public enterprises such as now exist in municipal and federal power, public transport, health and education will prove appropriate for some situations in some time periods, not in others. Public development banking, both for lending of money directly to innovative firms, or for providing capital improvements necessary for private development, like road extensions, harbor improvements, site preparation, and so forth, will be helpful in other situations. Deregulation and privatization will be a useful remedy in still other cases.

In conclusion the long-term shift in our metropolitan economy from its old concentration on manufactures to its new more diversified form of manufacturing with many services offers us a great deal of profit with which to work. To take advantage of this new opportunity we must face up to what we know to be the consequences of our existing economy and tackle its shortcomings on an item-by-item basis: land, food, housing, health, education, transportation, and energy. We can do better with our mixed public and private economy than we have done in the past, only if we move forward with the full knowledge that times change rapidly, that today's solutions will often be tomorrow's problems, and that many times we will fail. If we are willing to accept these conditions we can make Boston, and the United States, a much better place for everyone to live.

V.

The Peaceable Kingdom

Those of you who have been regularly attending these lectures may, by now, have picked up the central thread which for me runs through all the topics we have touched upon. It is a line which draws together the overall patterns that city dwellers make by their billions of individual decisions. Our beginning concept—Boston as a human settlement—orders us to find the social and economic patterns which six million Americans make when they gather about a place called Boston.

Such a focus upon human affairs inevitably confronts the tension between the goals of individuals and the outcomes of their myriad actions. Each person strives to earn what he can, each firm works for its own profit, each agency of government and each philanthropic organization does what it can to survive and to grow. The metropolitan sum of all these individual and corporate efforts, though each may be without malice towards its neighbors, is often destructive to the whole.

My introduction to this paradox came from studying, for my book, *Streetcar Suburbs,* the process whereby Roxbury, West Roxbury, and Dorchester were built at the end of the nineteenth century. In those towns at that time, individual builders and home buyers sought to escape the crowded city, to enjoy some of the pleasures and benefits of small-town life, and the amenities of a lightly settled countryside. The sum of thirty years of these individual escapes added up to the destruction of both the community style and the landscape amenities they all sought. The same process of destruction through growth reaches today to the shores of Cape Cod and Rhode Island, and to the mountains of New Hampshire.

The family is likewise ruled by the same kind of conflicts. The family group makes demands upon the father, mother, and children, and these individuals often perceive these demands as destructive of their own personal needs. Often they are. The essence of the recent women's movement is a call for changes in the rules of families, a call for the reordering of the list of demands which husbands and children may legitimately make upon wives and mothers.

In the last two lectures on the Boston economy we noted the general result of individual employer and employee actions upon the families of the entire Boston metropolis. Although the welfare of each person and each family depends upon the conditions and returns of work, chronic unemployment and wages below the current living standard have ruled Boston since the twenties. Although real income for all Bostonians has risen about two and a half times in fifty years, our customary wage scales and modes of employment hold at least a third of the population in shameful poverty. The affluent poverties of the 1970's in turn poison almost every aspect of group life among us, just as the older subsistence poverties did.

The conflicts between individual goals and group needs can never be ended, they are basic to living in groups, they are the essence of city life. Nor should we imagine that somewhere a perfect harmony awaits us, or that science will someday discover a cure for this tension. Rather our choice is limited to altering the rules for citizens, corporations, institutions, and governments, so that the sum of their individual undertakings creates a human settlement which approximates our goal of balances between the individual and the settlement itself.

Following this reasoning, I have over the years been forced to conclude that there is something we all like about holding one third of our fellow citizens in relative poverty. We like the contrast between the freedom, power, and luxury of the executive and the narrow discipline imposed by the wages of a clerk, stenographer, or millhand. We like slums, as well as suburbs, that is why we keep building both. It all must seem to us the correct order for a city, something just and proper.

Should we tire of the human destruction our metropolitan system creates, should we change our goals for the economy of our metropolis, should we wish to discard our steep hierarchy of power, knowledge, and wealth in favor of a more even distribution of these resources, then in doing so we would enjoy two advantages our fathers and grandfathers lacked.

We have much more wealth than they to distribute among ourselves.

We also have now sufficient knowledge and technique, at least in those aspects of human affairs which are narrowly economic, to experiment, and to test and repair our experiments quickly, accurately, and cheaply. We are the beneficiaries of the very complexity and variety which our metropolitan economy creates. Such an economy offers us a wide range of alternatives, alternatives as numerous as the parts of the economy itself.

We could harness that variety and complexity to building a more humane metropolitan economy if we wished.

In our relationships between our human settlement and its natural environments we meet again the same conflict between individuals and the group. The fast car becomes crawling traffic, downtown and suburban traffic become metropolitan air pollution, and air pollution kills and injures plants, animals, and people. Or, six million glasses of water and one million washing machines inevitably become a public water system, and public water systems quickly turn into sewage outflows, and untreated sewage returns to attack the plants, animals, and people again.

The water cycles of urban man, although still imperfectly mapped, have been subjects for study for a century, but the consequences of air pollution have, until recent years, been more the province of artists who deal in fogs and smoke, than a concern for scientists. We have attended to the economic plants, their predators and diseases, corn and its borers, tobacco and its mosaics, but only in the last few years have we given much thought to the plants, fish, birds, and animals of the metropolis.

The early twentieth-century union of conservationists, foresters, naturalists, and hunters has generated a body of information and skill in the management of the wildlife in backwoods America, but with the exception of our endless war with the rat, we lack data, theory, and technique for the management of the metropolitan natural environment. When startling crises, like the epidemics of yellow fever, cholera, and typhoid of the nineteenth century, or the deaths caused by the proliferation of toxic substances in the twentieth, force the subject upon us, only then have we turned our attention to the natural systems which interact with urban man. Characteristically, our society turns to the subject with all the enthusiasm of a man going down the stairs to clean out his cellar, not with the anticipation of the man gathering up his tools to plant a garden.

At the root of our ignorance and neglect of urban nature lie deep traditions of thought and feeling wherein we separate ourselves from the rest of the natural kingdom. We do not, as city dwellers, ordinarily think of ourselves as participants in the myriad natural systems which make up the metropolis. Rather we see ourselves as people dwelling in a man-made environment of buildings, streets, and highways. From our customary position in this built environment we gaze outwards at landscapes —at yards, street trees, parks, golf courses, forests, and seashores. Notice, we have a special word for looking at nature: "landscape." The landscape is where nature is, it is apart from us, it is not inside us, we are not part of it.

Just as we chose not to see the suburb as the inevitable product of the same human settlement as the slum, so we do not see ourselves as part of metropolitan nature. Our politics reflect this emotional division. Those concerned with conservation and wildlife are often opposed to spending money on welfare, minimum wages, or urban rebuilding, while advocates of such man-centered policies often have little taste for voting money for parks or forests. We have nature politicians, and people politicians.

I am sorry to have to report to you that in this folly, as in the absurdities of our advanced economy, we in Boston must be willing to accept the blame for an early leadership role. We carry with us, not any longer as Bostonians but today as urban Americans, modern, and secularized (should I have said decayed?) religious traditions which give us a peculiar and isolated view of ourselves as creatures apart from the common run of God's creations.

One branch of this religious tradition is inescapable in today's metropolis of science and machines. It is the quite understandable, if unjustified, point of view which not only places man at the center of the universe, but also makes him lord of it all as well. In the very opening chapter of the Bible this man-centeredness is certified as an injunction from God to Adam and Eve. "And God blessed them, and God said unto them, Be fruitful, and multiply, and replenish the earth, and subdue it: and have dominion over the fish of the sea, and over the fowl of the air, and over every living thing that moveth upon the earth." (Genesis, 1:28)

Those of you with a taste for theological disputation might well argue that the subsequent fall from grace constituted an implied revocation of this old hunting license, and that it has been invalid ever since Adam and Eve ate the apple. I favor such an interpretation. In any case we have so multiplied and so modified the earth that the old adversary relationship to nature is now a dangerous absurdity. It is a set of ideas which threatens human life itself.

An alternative branch of our religious tradition reaches us by way of Ralph Waldo Emerson, Henry David Thoreau and the spread of Transcendentalism. Transcendentalism was itself a Boston variant of a very widespread and popular late eighteenth- and early nineteenth-century romantic attitude towards God and nature. Transcendentalists, and many of their contemporaries, thought contact with nature to be a reliable source of religious experience. A moving and elevated emotional state awaited those who contemplated a wild setting, or at least a setting which had not been too obviously, or too recently, altered by man's work. A harmless doctrine on its face, in popular use it reinforced commonplace secular divisions of human life and society. Transcendentalists and romantic nature viewers contrasted city with country, man with nature, very much to the disadvantage of both city and man. The partiality, the artificiality, the evil of man (all consequences to be expected once we departed from Eden) stood in embarrassing contrast to the completeness, timelessness, beauty, and even grandeur of nature.

Today, to our modern ears, Thoreau sounds the best of the group because his careful observations of nature restrain his religious enthusiasm. For instance, he writes of the sudden warmth of spring in anticipation of summer:

> It is impossible to remember a week ago. A river of Lethe flows with many windings the year through, separating one season from another. The heavens for a few days have been lost. It has been a sort of *paradise* instead. As with the seashore, so it is with the universal earthshore, not in summer can you look far into the ocean of the ether. They who come to this world as to a watering-place in the summer for coolness and luxury never get the far and fine November views of heaven. Is not all the summer akin to a paradise? We have to bathe in ponds to brace ourselves. The earth is blue now,—the near hills, in this haze. (May 9, 1852, *Journal*)

Note in this carefully worked-out piece on the feeling of summer heat, the characteristic Boston Puritan view of sensuality. Summer is a paradise, but one cannot really experience God until the cold of November. This anti-sensual tradition which is so common among us here accounts for a good deal of the anger which is also a quality of Boston people throughout history. We have been experiencing it once again in our recent racial angers.

Transcendentalism and romanticism have long since died as movements, but their influence flows directly into us. They inspired Frederick Law Olmsted, the urban park designer. His romantic approach to nature is still visible in the graceful designs of Franklin Park and the Muddy River and Jamaica Pond string of parks. According to experts on Olmsted like Laura Wood Roper and Albert Fein, many of the parks in the cities of the United States, and many of our state and national parks and forests owe their inception to this same doctrine.

The rustic signs and awkward structures of our national parks and forests find inspiration for their ugliness in a mistaken attempt to subordinate the built and the man-made to the unbuilt and the God-made. Recently this divided view of man and nature has enjoyed a tremendous revival. Our ecological scientists, people like the late Rachel Carson, were inspired by it; the Audubon Society and the Sierra Clubs are propsering, and scratch a birdwatcher or a backpacker and chances are that beneath the patina of human courtesy you will find the basic misanthropy which this divided view of the world implies.

By encouraging people to use nature as an escape, by not seeing man everywhere in nature, and nature everywhere in man, this divided view is a life-destroying force among us. Thoreau did not dwell on the social implications of the Irishman's railside shack which he dismantled to build his

Fig. V-1
Edward Hicks,
"Peaceable Kingdom"
(oil on canvas), 1844

Courtesy of the Abby Aldrich Rockefeller Folk Art Collection.

cabin; no more do we in our revival of enthusiasm for things wild, include the Roxbury rat in our list of interesting creatures. The nineteenth-century trainloads of visitors to the White Mountains and the Adirondacks looked at the mountains and lakes and quite properly deplored contemporary methods of lumbering; they did not see the lumbercamps. So today we pass through the signboard jungle of Route 28, or Route 6 towards the beautiful Cape Cod seashore without more complicated thoughts than perhaps an anger that commercialism is ruining a beautiful landscape. So it is.

Behind these popular, and now even somewhat politically powerful sentiments, lies yet another emotion, and it too has been living in our religious tradition. This variant, which also picks up the longing for a return to Eden, stresses man's harmony with nature, not his conquest of it or separation from it. That harmony is equated with peace among men. I refer to Isaiah's restatement of the traditional welcoming of a new king of the Jews. On the occasion of the coming to the throne of a new king, Isaiah wrote some lines which were later interpreted as predicting the coming of Christ, and which were in the early years of the nineteenth century very popular in our country of Bible-reading farmers. He painted a picture of his hopes for a virtuous king. The governance of such a king would bring a peaceable kingdom in which wars among men would cease, and the conflicts between man and nature, begun at the Fall, would end:

> The wolf also shall dwell with the lamb, and the leopard shall lie down with the kid; and the calf and the young lion and the fatling together; and a little child shall lead them.
> And the cow and the bear shall feed; their young ones shall lie down together: and the lion shall eat straw like the ox.
> And the sucking child shall play on the hole of the asp, and the weaned child shall put his hand on the cockatrice' den. (Isaiah, 11:6-8)

An American folk painter, a popular Quaker preacher, Edward Hicks of Newtown, Pennsylvania (1780-1849), found time between painting signs, furniture, clocks, and carriages to paint fifty versions of Isaiah's royal compliment. I believe the Boston Museum of Fine Arts owns one copy.

Compare in your mind this sentimental picture by Hicks (Fig. V-1) to the sentimental nature posters of our day. Hardly an office is now without its prints and photographs of wild nature, sunsets, fall foliage, rushing brooks, mountains, and gentle animals. The appeal to the emotions of longing for peace and harmony is the same, but Hicks and his audience were much closer to the Biblical passage. In this version of his Peaceable Kingdom he put Quakers and Indians into the scene. The images were added to make a direct reference to Isaiah. By his putting man in a picture expressing the universal feeling of longing for peace and harmony, Hicks imitates Isaiah who preceded his nature images by a call for a just and wise king.

The Biblical metaphor symbolizes the condition precedent for any successful environmental thinking. A modern metropolitan American cannot escape man and the city for a fantasy landscape. Instead we must all do our best to join heart and mind in seeking the answers to two interlocking questions:

First, what is the fitting natural environment for a natural man?

Second, what is a fitting human settlement for nature and natural man?

In answering the first question about the natural setting for man, our neglect of environmental science exposes us to all the hazards of ignorance. We do, however, possess in our public-health traditions a strategy for seeking safety despite the uncertainties of ignorance. It is the equivalent to the movement for measurement and experimentation as devices to cope with the uncertainties of economic change.

In answering the second question about the design of a fitting human settlement for natural man, and other living things, the issue of goals is paramount. A few minima are clear, but beyond these, our alternatives depend very much upon what sort of a metropolitan world we want to live in.

The minima may be apparent, but they are not easy to achieve. Clearly we have gained little from our escapist efforts if the beautiful romantic design of Franklin Park is rendered almost unusable by youthful barbarism, and class and racial warfare. Similarly it will profit us little if we build a harmonious metropolis here in Boston, only to have it impoverished by armaments, or destroyed by atomic warfare.

For the subtler and more complex issues of seeking appropriate goals for ourselves, let us examine the current Boston metropolis and look at what we have been doing with our relationships to nature and our natural selves. In this lecture we will focus upon the central cities, the most densely populated areas of the metropolis. In the next lecture we will survey Boston as a whole.

Recall the LANDSAT satellite photographs of the region (Figs. I-2 and I-3). Boston, Providence, Haverhill, Lawrence, Lowell, Manchester, Brockton, Taunton, and Fall River appeared as small gray clearings in the metropolitan forest.

These core cities are very special environments, for man, and for all other living things. They are something like deserts, but they concentrate such an abundance of food that man and all the other species who dwell here live at higher densities than in any other environments in the world.

The climate in the core cities differs from the rest of the metropolis. You must recall the television forecaster's phrase—"Tonight the temperature in Boston will be in the thirties, in the twenties in the suburbs. . . ." The differential stands day and night, all year long. Central city temperatures are about ten degrees above the normals for the region because the concentration of people, lights, heating, automobiles, factories, and power plants, create waves of extra heat here. During the day the unshaded absorption of pavements and buildings increases this effect, and these surfaces act like radiators at night. We enjoy the difference during the winter, it cuts our fuel bills, turns marginal snows to rain, and promotes melting. In short it gives us the advantages of cows huddled in a winter barn, it may not smell so good, but it beats standing out in the wind. In summer we suffer from the heat, and from the loss of wind speed caused by the obstruction of buildings. In response we make things worse by putting a peak demand upon our power plants, and heating up the streets with our office, store, home and automobile airconditioners.

The pollution of the air is most intense in the central cities too. The dust, smoke particles, and exhaust gasses capture moisture, and fogs and rain showers shroud the city more often than the suburbs or countryside. The beautiful scenes of the English painter, Turner, owe their inspiration to the special fogs of London, fogs created by millions of coal-burning stoves. The extra moisture does not, however, improve the lot of urban plantlife. It is acid, and since it causes only fogs and showers, it does not soak the ground. From the point of view of plants, the city is very much a desert, not as cold at night as the real article, but dry, and made especially inhospitable by paving and noxious air. Authorities such as Reid A. Bryson and John E. Kutzbach in *Air Pollution,* and Thomas R. Detwyler and Melvin G. Marcus in *Urbanization and the Environment* describe and document these features of the urban environment.

Nancy Page and Richard Weaver of the Arnold Arboretum have written an enthusiastic and wonderfully informative illustrated book on the wild plants of Boston, *Wild Plants in the City.* I recommend it to you as a guidebook for what can be seen and enjoyed in our central cities. In general most of our urban plants are not native to the United States but are accidental imports from Europe and Asia. They have been growing with urban man since ancient times, and they have adapted to withstand bad soil, heat in summer, and cold and exposure to wind in winter. Like all urban dwellers, human, insect, and animal, they have an enormous reproductive capacity, being plants which spread quickly by a vast proliferation of seeds.

Best known among us is the *Ailanthus altisima,* the Tree of Heaven, the tree Betty Smith made famous as the tree that grows in Brooklyn. It can still be found as a wild forest tree in China, but it is an urban plant here. Considered for many years an ornamental because of its profusion of spring flowers, it was imported to Boston by China traders at the end of the eighteenth century, and by mid-nineteenth century it was a popular seller at nurseries. In the spring winds its seeds make showers, and by this fecundity the tree finds the cracks and corners of the leftover places of the city.

Although hardiness and rapid growth make it an ideal shade tree for city streets, the *Ailanthus* does not meet our exacting specifications. Its wood is soft and pulpy, so its limbs break in winter icestorms. Its staminate flowers and sap give off a bad smell (it is sometimes known as stinkweed). Altogether, the tree is regarded as too messy to suit us. Obviously, as John Rublowsky says in *Nature in the City,* the condition of our cars parked along the curb is of more importance to us than our shade as pedestrians, or the cooling of our porches and houses.

In fact the whole idea that our streets ought to be shaded at all is an innovation for which we can thank the romantic view of nature. During the seventeenth, eighteenth and early nineteenth centuries street trees were not thought to be objects for public concern. When Charles Dickens visited Boston in 1841 he did not admire the canopies of spreading chestnuts and elms, instead, he remarks in *American Notes* upon the cheerful brightness of the signs which decorated the shops and houses. The streets of Beacon Hill, laid out as a fashionable development fitting to the latest taste, did not anticipate street trees. After all, such trees would lessen the effect of the homebuyers' imposing frontage. In time, however, the romantic view gained ground, and many of Boston's streets were planted. Old photographs, as in the Boston 200 Neighborhood Series, of East Boston, Roxbury, and the Back Bay, show the native elm especially as a pleasant meliorator of the urban climate.

Since 1920 the demands of the automobile have increasingly narrowed the possible urban environments for trees. Paved streets and sidewalks of cement and tar cut off the water and covered formerly open earth spaces (most streets were not paved until the auto) and horse manure no longer nourished the soil. Blights, for which the city is in no way responsible, carried off the chestnut and the elm; the horse chestnut came to be considered too messy for our street parking, and many native oaks and maples are just too big, or don't thrive in pavements and polluted air.

Given the new constraints, and the new rules that street trees must not wrench the pipes in the ground, nor wear the wires in the air, our search for urban trees is a very specialized search indeed. We meet our old friend, impoverishment through progress, once again in this subject. The London plane tree is a good example of today's urban nature. It is a cross between an Oriental and a native American sycamore. Narrower than the American plant, its branches are less of a challenge to trucks and overhead wires. Its roots are also shallower than its American parent, so that it doesn't grab pipes and cables buried beneath it, and it also better captures the water from showers and brief rains than its deep-rooted relative.

The Asiatic sycamore was imported into England in 1562, the American in 1636. The two were crossed and wealthy English gentlemen grew the hybrid on their estates. Thence it migrated to London's parks and streets and in time its special ability to withstand air pollution manifested itself. Since World War II the London plane tree has been widely planted here in Boston, and has become the New York street and park tree, where, Rublowsky reports, it is known as the buttonball for its round seed balls.

A recent article in the *Scientific American*, by Thomas S. Elias and Howard C. Irwin, reviews the current campaign to find a range of not-too-large and not-too-small, salt-resistant, pollution-proof, drought-withstanding, wind-safe, ice-bearing, neat but ornamental, urban trees. Selective breeding and hybridization are the current devices used by scientists and nurserymen to construct such natural wonders. Surely we could have been saved such trouble and expense if only Henry Thoreau had mentioned laminated fiberglass in his *Walden*. Or, we could change our specifications for nature.

Success in the urban animal and bird world depends upon being like man, but it is essential that one be small, so one doesn't get in man's way. But like humans and urban plants, successful animals and birds possess a great fecundity. Like man too they are smart and aggressive, omnivorous, and very flexible in living quarters. Our native raccoon, gray squirrel, and skunk meet these specifications, as do the blue jay and herring gull. Like man a successful urban animal or bird can use the city to escape its wilderness predators—the skunk escapes the fox, the sparrow the hawk; while the abundance of food in the city makes disease, overpopulation, and automobiles the principal dangers to life. Don Gill and Penelope Bonnett discuss such animals in their book, *Nature in the Urban Landscape*.

Of all the urban mammals, the Norway rat most resembles man, and is therefore best suited to city life. His relatives are the test subjects we employ when we want to determine if a new drug is safe for us to use on ourselves, and a recent report by David E. Davis on the overcrowding of Norway rats has been widely cited as a definitive model for human behavior.

An immigrant who came to America with the first European settlers, the Norway rat is smart and aggressive. He has some capacities for group life, hence the phrase "rat pack," and there have been reports of rats forming into armies a mile long to migrate across the corn fields of southern Illinois. Unlike most of us, the rodent is primarily a nocturnal animal only foraging by day when forced to by overpopulation and starvation. The rule of thumb of field workers estimates that when you see one rat there are twenty nearby.

William B. Jackson reports that a rat forages at night over a range of about 100-150 yards from its nest. His feeding habits and his practice of burrowing under trash and old lumber and nesting in the cracks of cellars keep him out of people's way. An omnivorous eater whose diet today consists largely of garbage, he, like the housemouse, the English sparrow, the cockroach, and the ant, is a useful creature who cleans up after us. So well adapted to man's ways is he that the rat can be found wherever man dwells, except in the Arctic. Here in our central city there is supposed to be one rat for every Bostonian.

The Norway rat has only one natural predator—us. Despite his contribution to urban recycling he makes a dangerous neighbor. The vector and carrier of typhus and bubonic plague (20 cases, United States 1976) and other diseases, in the past the rat has contributed to massive die-offs of human beings. Fortunately the Boston rats have not been infected with rabies for the past twenty years, but this danger is always present because in the suburbs and countryside dwell the foxes and skunks, our native pool of rabies bearers. When hungry, rats bite people, especially children, and the bites are painful and cause a feverish infection. Also contact with rat feces and urine causes fevers in humans. (Data on Boston's rats come from Ronald Jones and Albert Storms of Boston City Hospital Environmental Health Improvement Program.)

The control of rats does not depend upon the science of chemistry. Rather the rat population grows and shrinks according to human behavior. During the nineteenth century when Boston's slums were their most crowded and worst maintained, and when horses and stables were everywhere in the city, the rats prospered. Subsequently improvements in the management of trash and garbage, the cleaning up of vacant lots, the relief of overcrowded housing, and the substitution of gasoline for oats has helped reduce the rat population of Boston by eliminating nesting places and cutting back the food supply.

Today, as in the past, the rats are not evenly distributed among us. Where people are poor, land care and housing maintenance are also poor, and city services are inadequate. As a result our economic customs find themselves mirrored in the rats' well-being. Currently a special team at the Boston City Hospital is endeavoring to reduce the rat population of Roxbury and Dorchester. Most of their effort is spent on social organization among the humans—finding and assisting block committees who supervise trash disposal, both municipal and private, and who try to force landlords to comply with our laws for building and yard maintenance. It is a slow and arduous process, so difficult because it runs against the economic grain of our society.

If the street tree is an issue of urban design for human comfort, and if the rat is an issue of human organization for human health, the central city bird population raises the question of how one wishes to relate to the other elements of nature which are neither a source of wealth nor safety.

Successful inner-city birds meet all the specifications we have discussed: they are omnivorous, quick, aggressive, flexible, not too large, and very fertile. Like most of the inner-city plants and animals, they too tend not to be natives of America, but birds who have found over centuries ecological niches in man's constructions. The pigeon is a rock dove which formerly roosted in cliffs and journeyed out each day to feed in farmers' fields. It now roosts in the corners and ledges of our bridges and buildings and feeds on the streets and in the parks of the city. The starling, which learned to roost in the cities and feed in suburban gardens and fields, performs a useful function for us by feeding on Japanese beetle grubs in suburban lawns. Only as recently as 80 years ago did some starlings learn to both nest and forage all-year-round in the city.

My favorite among these successful central city immigrants is the house sparrow, or English sparrow as we often call it. It can now be heard giving its regular loud chirps from the vines and ledges of our buildings, calling for its mate. We see it in small flocks which suddenly drop down to the ground in the parks and yards of the city. A brown, and during late winter and early spring, a very dirty small bird, the male can be identified by its large black front bib and white cheeks. It has the thick bill of a seed eater, for such is its exurban habit, but like man the house sparrow will eat most anything. A systematic study of the contents of the stomachs of these birds, reported by D. Summers-Smith in *The House Sparrow,* revealed 838 different identifiable food items. Because it was not originally a ground feeder it has not yet learned to walk, but hops about, a style which I find adds to its repertoire of entertainment.

Because the bird was remembered with fondness from the old country it was introduced into Brooklyn in 1851. In that decade there were numerous other importations along the east coast, including one in Boston. By 1888 house sparrows had so multiplied that they covered almost all of the continental United States and today it is estimated that there is one house sparrow for every five Americans (approximately 40 million). Like the rat this sparrow reached its population peak in the horse era, feeding on street grain and the incompletely digested oats in horse manure.

A smart, aggressive bird, it has been shown in learning tests to be the equal of the pigeon and the rat, and it has used this talent to find food and nests everywhere. It eats bugs trapped in car radiators, and in London learned to puncture the foil caps of milk bottles which sat on doorsteps after delivery and before people woke up to take them inside. It is not as successful a panhandler as the pigeon, but there are sparrow feeders in our parks. Most of its urban food consists of urban insects and man's leftovers. Like the rat too the sparrow has some social capacities. Adults in the small spring flocks will feed others' fledglings while the parents are off foraging for food, or if the parents have died.

In the country, according to Summers-Smith, the house sparrow lives at a density of about one sparrow for every ten acres, in dense urban settlements with parks it reaches a density forty times its rural habit. In short, the house sparrow can be used as a measure of urbanization. Two recent articles, one by Charles F. Walcutt on the changing bird composition of Cambridge, Massachusetts since 1860, the other a careful study of changes brought about by the building of Columbia, Maryland, by Aelred D. Geis, recount the process whereby building by man reduced the variety of birds which can live in an area. As building goes on the environment becomes narrower and narrower and the specialized urban birds move in to replace the much wider variety of the former residents.

This process, documented for birds, can serve us as a general model for our urban relations with the rest of the natural kingdom. As we increase the built environment the total numbers, the total populations of plants, insects, animals, and birds which occupy a space may not decline, indeed they may increase, but the *variety* of species will fall off very sharply. In a word as we humans urbanize, we create more and more of a sameness, less of a variety.

Because our cities are also the products of our economy there is a corollary to the general rule of man's interaction with the rest of nature. Within the urban settlement itself as poverty among humans increases, the variety of other species decreases. I suppose the long-eroded lands of China are the most dramatic examples of this corollary, but here in our city the principle holds and can be observed. In our poorest neighborhoods vacant lots replace gardens, parks are neglected or are absent, street trees inherited from a former time are abused and not replaced; rats, mice, roaches, and ants multiply.

Here we strike at the center of our question about fitting goals for natural man living with nature. Much of the current conservation politics, like much of American politics, employs scare tactics. Instead of the Russians, the enemy is the rat. In the latter case the scare seems appropriate, but it is hard to make a scare case from a narrow view of human health and safety. Although we have drastically limited the varieties of plants, animals and birds in the city, we are not, as far as anyone can reasonably tell, in danger for our lives. Instead we confront in this question of our goals the questions raised by the story of Eden and the religious longings of the romantics and Transcendentalists.

Living in a modern secular society we are nothing if not creatures of nature. Therefore questions about our place in nature are inescapable. In reviewing the history and conditions of our central city we have been examining the most dramatic case of our widespread power and intervention. As creatures of nature we have sharply reduced the varieties of other species we live among, we have imported foreign plants and birds, and we are busy breeding and hybridizing trees and plants. Conditions are not otherwise in the suburbs, or throughout the metropolis. We are today, as we have been for a long time, the major force for change to which all the other members of the natural kingdom must adapt. To a remarkable degree we are the architects of our natural, as well as of our built world.

In conclusion let me summarize our current plight in the old theological terms. Since the Creation man has had to get used to receiving a lot of bad news. Throughout most of human history that news took the form of one dispatch after another which said that God was alive, but he wasn't helping. A few years ago some of our theologians announced that they had discovered that God was dead. As I read our natural history and environmental literature still worse news is coming over the wire—we are God.

VI.

The Metropolitan Zoo

In considering the relationship between our human settlement and metropolitan nature we concentrated in the last lecture upon the extreme case, upon the conditions in our most densely settled areas, the central cities of the region. By reviewing briefly the histories of some typical urban species, the *Ailanthus*, the London plane tree, the rat, and the house sparrow, it became evident that our actions dominated the environment and that our ways of urban living set the boundaries for all the species which dwell among us.

To a degree that I find frightening, frightening since we are after all a fallible species ourselves, we have taken over the role of God: we not only build our cities, but populate the earth with plants, animals, birds, and insects.

While God seems to have taken delight in the variety of His creations, our laws for nature operate in quite the opposite way. As the density of our settlement increases, the variety of other species declines. The number of living things sharing our urban space may not be less in our central cities than in the suburbs or the country; it may even be greater because in the city we leave so much food around, but the list of species which thrive in the city is short. The greater variety of species which are not adapted to city environments disappears as we build. The density of the human animal brings a sameness of environments.

In our review of urban natural history we also discovered a corollary to the species law of urban nature. Namely, human wealth and natural variety bear a positive relationship to each other. In the wealthy sections of our cities the variety of species is the greatest, in the poor sections narrowed environments restrict the species variety.

The way we really live in Boston is such that we restrict the list of species which can live among us. We reduce the range of life far below what our hot summers, cold winters, or sandy and stony soil can bear.

The sharp decline in the density of Boston's core cities since 1920 offers a fresh opportunity to relieve the natural monotony our fathers built. We have opportunities for parks where houses have been abandoned, we have opportunities to adapt our highway borders into pathways for birds and animals, and we have opportunities for a multiplicity of suburban and rural designs which could place emphasis on the heterogeneity of the environments which exist in our part of New England. We need not continue to live in a world of either well-tended or abused deserts.

Although we do have a fresh chance to alter our life in nature, our traditional modes of thinking make it difficult for us to set goals for public action. Our debate tends to be narrowly economic, even in this field. If someone can show that air pollution causes some measurable incidence of disease, hospital costs, or work days lost, then, albeit reluctantly, public remedies for air pollution gain a hearing. If subdivisions with rhododendrons and lawns seem to sell better than subdivisions with privet and driveways then rhododendrons and lawns will multiply among us.

Yet debate which rests upon casting up the economic losses against the gains will not carry us very far in setting goals for our metropolitan natural life. Too many decisions of design and policy—whether they be for parking lots, subdivisions, or open space—concern issues which don't fit easily into even the most sophisticated cost-benefit analysis. When we come to this part of the argument we alternate between asking too little or too much of ourselves. If we are opposed to some program we belittle it as being overburdened with mere amenities, or top-heavy with "aesthetics." If, on the other hand, we favor some program we make outrageous claims for the life-sustaining properties of pine groves, or the essential role of some swamp in the maintenance of a vast chain of being.

Our incapacity to think clearly in such matters grows out of a long-standing confusion. The bulldozer and the naturalist are old opponents among us, and as Americans we carry these opposites in our heads as commonly as we drive cars and flock to seashores and the mountains.

In the last lecture we looked briefly into our religious traditions to find the roots of our confused thinking about nature. We found echoes of the present enthusiasms for both reckless engineering, and sentimental views of nature in the Bible. We traced the polar injunctions of the Old Testament through the romantics and the Transcendentalists of Boston. We even detected in a nature passage of Thoreau that special antisensuality which has been such a curse to thought and life here in Boston.

The accomplishments of both schools lie all about: The wonders of modern science and engineering, and the beautiful city, state, and federal parks and forests of the romantics. But the peculiar attitude towards man and nature which dominates the two modes of thought currently impoverishes us. The sterility and inhumanity of much of the built environment is the work of the first school, the ruthless hostility to cities, and the misanthropy of much public policy is the work of the second.

In seeking a new attitude and in setting fresh goals for our relationships with metropolitan nature it seems most profitable to me to start with what we know best—to start with natural man in the city. Although neither our scientists nor our naturalists have concentrated here, as ordinary citizens we know most about this world: we live in it.

When we are at our best in this environment, what is our behavior as human animals? When we are sitting in the Boston Common, or walking down a busy street, or stopping for a moment in our shopping and errands, or are looking into our neighbors' windows and back yards, our curiosity about our fellow human beings is a great source of pleasure. As a visible urban species we are tall and short, thin and fat, young and old, quick and slow, happy and careworn, straight and broken, and all shades of a palette which runs from pink to dark brown. This variety produces a range of emotions among us from jealousy and fear to wonder and delight. However the emotions come towards us, the overall effect is pleasure, a delight in the recognition of human life itself. It is especially an urban pleasure, but it can be found to some degree wherever human beings congregate—and because we are that kind of animal we always do congregate. We even have a slightly deprecatory term which we use to soften the shock of recognition which comes with this experience—we call ourselves "the human zoo." And if you are for some reason unable to recognize yourself as part of that zoo, you are not ready for the fall foliage, or the view from the mountain, and even less are you prepared to interpret the meaning of what appears on the stage of the microscope, or in the tracings on the plates of the high-energy accelerator.

Here, I think, lies a more promising approach to metropolitan nature than either the narrow accounting of our traditional science, or the religious longings of our wilderness enthusiasts. It is only a matter of degree, not kind, which characterizes our pleasure in living with people and our pleasure in living with the house sparrow, the pigeon, or even our enemy the rat. We cannot argue on health and economic grounds that we would be worse off without these creatures. We could get on without them, just as we get on without the millions of species which have become extinct. No more can the citizens of Wellesley argue that the metropolis would fail, or be economically handicapped without them.

Our urban experience tells us that the necessity for variety in both nature and natural man is the same. We are at a certain point in natural and social evolution where we have a definite list of species to live with. The argument is the same for adding bobwhites to sparrows, and hickories to *Ailanthus*, as it is for including Wellesley in our design for the metropolis. Our life is impoverished if we unnecessarily restrict the variety of birds, plants, and animals we live among. So too are our suburbs impoverished for their lack of immigrants and blacks.

There are important issues of economy and health in any concern for metropolitan environments, and we should attend to these issues more than we have done in the past. There are issues of human justice among us which are urgent and demand immediate resolution. But intertwined with these issues stands the necessity for variety; it is a necessity we all know from our commonplace personal experiences as human animals who live in cities.

Nothing better demonstrates our unlooked-for stewardship of the natural world than our current struggles to manage the metropolitan atmosphere, water, and land. All were at various times in our local history infinite public goods which awaited our pleasure in consumption. Each demonstrates the inescapable conflicts between individual and group life which appeared first in these lectures when we examined the region's economy.

In the use of the resources of air, water, and land private wealth often generates public illth. Metropolitan air, indeed the atmosphere of the world, enters your carburetor and furnace as a public gift to your well-being, and it emerges from the exhaust pipe and chimney freighted with your poisonous gift to your fellow creatures. So long as we were few and cities small, such transactions were of no account, but beginning with industrial urbanization, in the nineteenth century, if not earlier, air ceased to be an infinite resource and became a subject for the management of man.

No subject calls more loudly for historical treatment than air quality because what we want to know is its history. How is the air changing? what makes it change? what are the effects of change? These are historical questions. Yet until comparatively recently air has not been viewed as a human problem and therefore it has not been subject to systematic study. Moreover, such historical studies as are possible (and a good deal about the past can at least be estimated) will be limited by the fact that so many aspects of the pre-1920 urban environment were lethal that the contribution of bad air will be hard to isolate.

In general it can be said with confidence that the nature of our air pollution in Boston, and much of the United States, has shifted since 1920. Prior to World War I the smoke of coal fires poisoned the urban atmosphere. With the spread of the automobile and the substitution of petroleum for heat and motive power the pollutants of oil have replaced the pollutants of coal. In technical terms our difficulties have shifted from particle pollution and sulfuric acid to all manner of gaseous pollutants. Moreover, recent successes in the control of industrial emissions, formerly a major source of particles, has brought those pollutants under control. By contrast we have moved only slightly in controlling the automobile so that the shift to gaseous contamination is intensified.

The history of public awareness and remedies follows the same trend. We began by looking with alarm at a few smoky city chimneys; we are now trying to monitor and control the lower atmosphere of the entire metropolis.

The first stage began in Boston in 1869, the second, about a century later, in 1960. According to an unpublished "History of Air Pollution Regulation in Massachusetts," in 1869 the Commonwealth created a state Board of Health, and smoke abatement was one of the many tasks assigned it. Other issues, however, the pressing demands of small pox vaccination, contaminated water, spoiled food, adulterated milk, and industrial health, occupied its attention and the Board accomplished little for the air. In 1901 and again in 1910 fresh legislation moved the responsibility for smoke to a Board of Gas and Electric Light Commissioners and over the years it sought to mitigate emissions from foundries and utilities. Noting the concentration of smoke the legislature created a smoke district, at first composed of Boston, Cambridge, Somerville, Everett, Chelsea, and Brookline, and later expanded the district to include 29 Boston cities and towns. In 1930 the staff was enlarged and its activity increased, but the Great Depression brought the repeal of the new law. This step backwards should warn us about the current arguments that we cannot afford to clean up our environment or keep to our standards for low-sulphur fuel or low-emission automobiles during a depression.

The basic problem for reformers during this first century lay in the absence of public awareness that air quality need be attended. Boston's peculiarly salubrious climate, and our absence of steel mills and oil refineries, kept our air at stable levels of illth, or at least produced no dramatic events until 1960.

Ours is the windiest big city in the United States, storm systems from Canada and the southwest regularly carry off, or wash down the contaminated local atmosphere. Since 1936 Boston has averaged only two extended intervals of air stagnation per year (four-day intervals), and in the fall season when cool night air creates long-lasting temperature inversions and hovering blankets of smog in other cities, our average inversions last less than six hours per day, as reported in Reid A. Bryson and John E. Kutzbach's study, *Air Pollution*. Dramatic events elsewhere were required to spur more effective local action.

A London fog of December 5-8, 1952, killed at

least 6,000 persons, and the deepening of Los Angeles smog became a standing joke in the press, radio, and the new medium, television. Encouraged by the opportunities of urban renewal, both St. Louis and Pittsburgh, heavy industry cities, instituted strict coal consumption programs. There, people who had been used to driving to work with their headlights on, suddenly discovered the morning sun. Growing citizen awareness of air pollution led Massachusetts to shift its agency responsibility from the utility board back to the state Board of Health. Then on May 13, 1960, an unusual fall-out of soot in South Boston brought a thoroughgoing reform and the institution of modern policies (Sec. 142B, Ch. 111, Gen. Laws).

The new division of sanitary engineering in the Massachusetts Department of Public Health (now the Massachusetts Department of Environmental Quality Engineering) abandoned the former concentration on the color of smoke coming out of chimneys and turned its attention instead to the quality of the air itself. It also defined pollution very broadly: a condition of the atmosphere that not only injured property or met the old law of nuisance, but also one which could potentially be injurious to human, animal, and plant life. The Federal Clean Air Act of 1970 and the setting up of the national Environmental Protection Agency completed the historical process in such a way that the national and regional scales of our atmosphere found their opposites in government agencies and policy.

The essence of our current situation is extreme political pain. The substitution of petroleum for coal, and the recent control of industrial emissions which have been quite successful, together have markedly improved the metropolitan atmosphere. Boston air, Providence air, and Worcester air smell better, and look clearer than ten and fifty years ago. Yet rising petroleum and gas prices threaten our regulations for low-sulfur fuels and bring demands for relaxation of controls on industry and automobiles. The current extended depression renews arguments used in the past to relax public controls over private behavior. Politically worse still, more thoroughgoing measures further to improve the air will require that we all alter styles of living to which we have just now become accustomed.

Although most businesses can pass on to their customers the costs of not polluting the atmosphere, many are reluctant to do so for fear of losing customers if their products become still more expensive. Finally what little we do know about air pollution suggests that we incur heavy costs in health and property if we do not maintain reasonably pure air, but we do not know enough to establish with certainty what the consequences of alternative levels of purity might be.

The mortality statistics are clear enough for humans: urban dwellers suffer disproportionately from a host of recorded disabilities. The complexity lies in the discovery, as Amasa B. Ford shows in *Urban Public Health,* that the probable causes of this urban differential are not single epidemics but intertwinings of disease, urban living styles, and urban environments. The exact contribution of each category is in doubt, and therefore measurement is as yet impossible. For example cigarette smoking is correlated with cancer and heart disease, so is urban air, and so is the frantic style of American urban life. The same tangle of multiple variables runs across the paths of toxic substances and industrial health.

In the past we have dealt successfully with such ignorance by following a public health strategy of general clean-up. Absent knowledge of the causal sequences we have tried to cleanse the city, provide fresh water, pure food, safe garbage and trash disposal, decent heating, and so forth. Each ingredient in the campaign was known to assist human life, none were known to be specific countermeasures for the elevated urban death rate.

What is known about air pollution points in the same direction. It is an urban phenomenon here in the Northeast. Consider two 1975 maps of sulfur dioxide (Fig. VI-1) and particle pollution (Fig. VI-2). Notice both maps look like density maps of the population of Massachusetts.

I do not have maps for the special outpourings of automobiles, carbon monoxide and hydrocarbons, but I have reviewed the 1975 monthly continuous monitoring reports, produced by the Massachusetts Department of Environmental Qual-

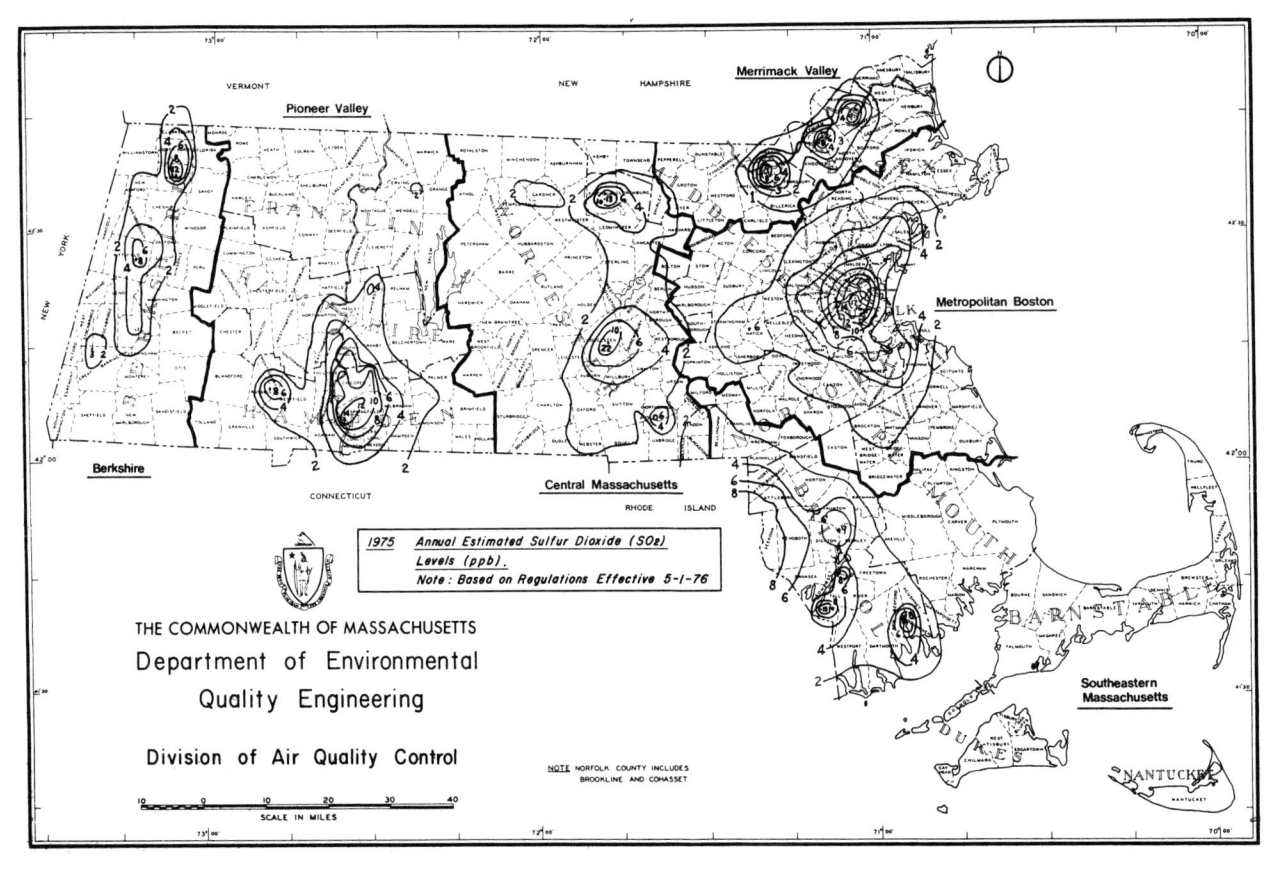

Fig. VI-1
Annual Estimated Sulfur Dioxide Levels, 1975

Source: Commonwealth of Massachusetts, Department of Environmental Quality Engineering.

ity Engineering, for eight stations in the Massachusetts part of the Boston BEA. Readings at Kenmore Square show the greatest concentration of pollutants, and Worcester and Waltham also are regional leaders. There are lesser variations, too. For instance ozone, which interacts with the nitrogen compounds in automobile exhaust, was especially prevalent in Quincy, Waltham, and Medfield, not Kenmore Square. In general however, the more people, the more traffic, and the more traffic the worse the air.

Taken all together the air monitors present us with an unhappy paradox. The very machine which enabled us to live at lowered densities and thereby disperse our pollution, generates intolerable levels of gaseous pollution over wide areas.

Currently several remedial actions are underway. The campaign against industrial emission continues, now concentrating on the hydrocarbons released into the air by evaporation of oil products in gasoline storage and industrial solvents. The magnitude of these sources came as a surprise to environmentalists who learned that the fumes escaping the oil storage yards and refineries of Los Angeles exceeded the outpourings from all the automobiles of that giant metropolis.

Governor Dukakis will introduce legislation in 1977 to revitalize the state's auto safety inspec-

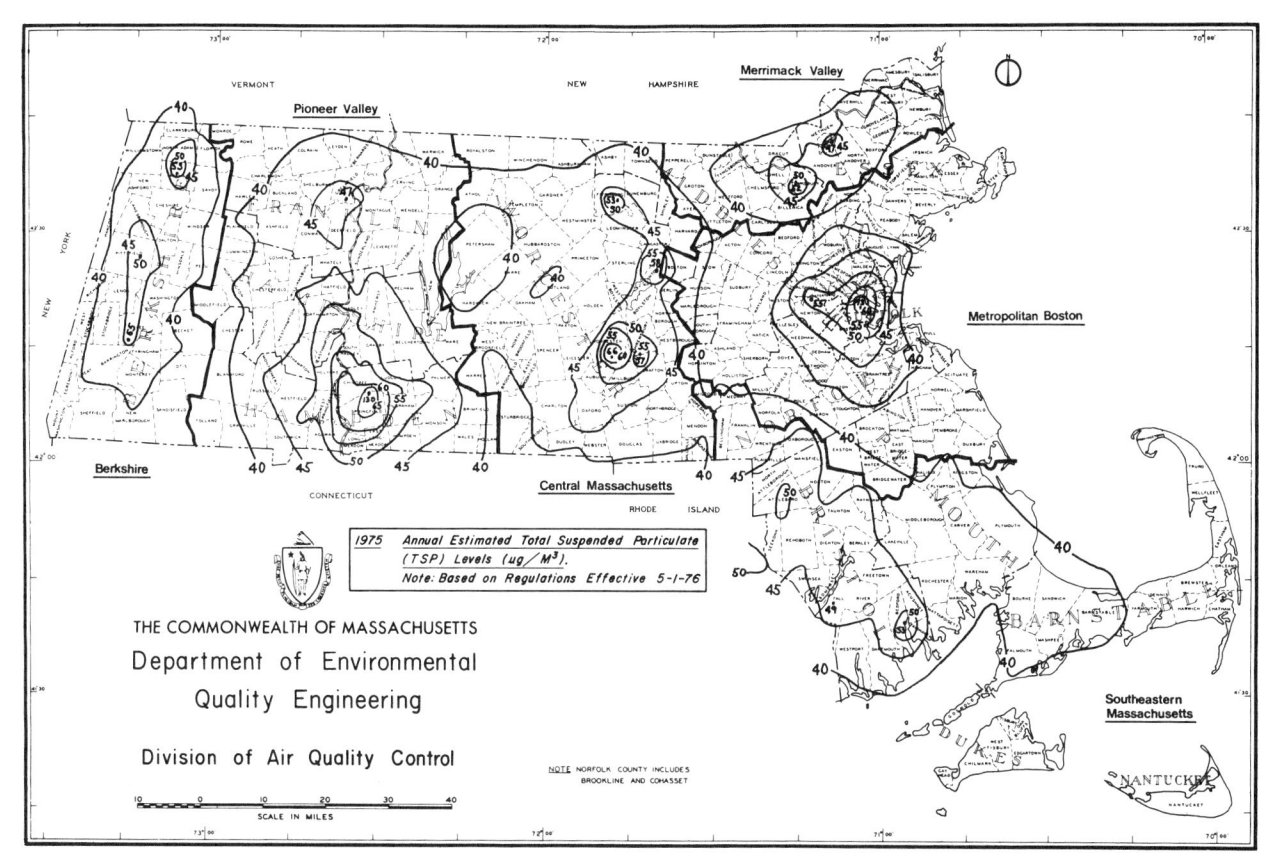

Fig. VI-2
Annual Estimated Total Suspended Particulate Levels, 1975

Source: Commonwealth of Massachusetts, Department of Environmental Quality Engineering.

tion system and to include with the tests, inspection of antipollution devices on cars. The hope is for a working program by 1979. Some building of bicycle paths may be forthcoming. One can purchase 180 miles of bicycle ways for the cost of half a mile of interstate highways, according to the Metropolitan Area Planning Council. These are small, if important steps, though they do not meet the private car problem head on.

We all own cars and we love to drive them. The wealthy among us, those with the greatest alternatives for various modes of transportation and amusement, far from setting an example of a new lifestyle, buy several cars, and even purchase power boats and airplanes as well. A huge industry, which tries to identify itself as the keystone of the nation's economy and the very embodiment of our culture, fights every attempt to limit the use of automobiles. As Barry Commoner says in *The Poverty of Power*, it was the auto manufacturers who after World War II introduced high-compression engines, a new design which added nitrogen compounds to the exhaust. Before this change, standard American cars were unable to produce such pollutants! Also by stubbornly clinging to this kind of engine the manufacturers have multiplied the antipollution devices on their cars, devices which we have to pay for, and which our mechanics neither understand nor appreciate. Extension of the MBTA is a logical partial step to reduce dependence on automobiles, but each extension meets the racism and class antagonisms of our local politics. Arlington is currently exhibiting its tenderness for the people of Boston and its concern for cleaning up the environment by vociferously resisting MBTA extension.

In these political conflicts over air pollution control, we confront the burdens of our stewardship of nature and the necessity to make choices among alternative styles of metropolitan life.

We bring to our problems with the management of the water of the metropolis, much more knowledge and experience than informs our air policies. In Boston we have the findings of more than a century of investigation, and the observation of a succession of engineering practices which date back to Boston's original construction, the Cochituate Lake supply of 1848. Knowledge and experience, however, have not sufficed to maintain a smooth-running metropolitan water system. In fact, our tradition of relying upon heavy regional engineering solutions seems to be laying an egg. Today water problems are cropping up all over the Boston BEA, and at the center, in the area inside Route 128, our past and present methods threaten us with the absurdity of transforming a polluted abundance into a sterile desert.

The effects of urbanization disrupt the normal cycles of water from New Hampshire to Rhode Island. Urban and industrial pollution contaminates all our rivers; the promiscuous salting of our highways poisons our wells and has forced several towns to abandon their own water systems and to hook onto the massive Metropolitan District Commission works. The MDC system is now short of water. On Cape Cod the boom in retirement and vacation homes doubled the demand for water over the past ten years and, if the current habits of waste disposal continue, either the salt water of the sea will be drawn into the Cape's wells, or the fresh water beneath the ground will become polluted. Experts for the Massachusetts Division of Water Resources guess that pollution will win the race.

The remedy for these conditions, like the remedy for most of our metropolitan problems, lies in much closer attention to the interactions between the behavior of the human settlement and the other natural systems of the region. And since we must in this field too decide what to do, the setting of appropriate goals again determines one's choice among alternatives.

Let us begin our investigation of our current situation by understanding a generalized model of how our water resources function. Then we can apply that model to a review of the history of our water management in the fifteen-mile core surrounding downtown Boston.

The central concept of a regional water system is the hydrologic budget. Though complicated in field measurement and estimation, it is a simple set of accounts which totals all the water coming into and going out of a region during a year. A general model for the whole BEA would begin with the water income—approximately 40 inches of rainfall per year. If there has been no drought for the previous years, so the ground is wet and the ponds full, then about half of that rain will flow out of the region through the brooks and rivers to the Atlantic Ocean. The other half evaporates back into the atmosphere, or is taken up by plants to make vegetative growth or passed out through the leaves of the plants themselves. The technical term for these two processes is "evapotranspiration."

Our contemporary forest cover gives us a valuable water asset. It has been estimated by Ernest M. Gould, Jr., that in the 1840's extensive cultivation reduced the forest cover to about 30 percent of the surface of the BEA, but the subsequent abandonment of farming has afforested the region once more, and trees and shrubs now blanket about 80 percent of the land. This vegetative cover slows evaporation by shading the ground while the roots stop erosion. Altogether the plants prevent sudden storm runoffs and floods, and release the water at a more even pace than fields would have. Together the forest and the abundant rainfall make Boston one of the favored places in the world; like the local weather, they are some of our few natural resources.

Urbanization alters the local hydrologic system by increasing runoff and by moving water around from place to place. As we cut down trees, roof over and pave the land through urban construction

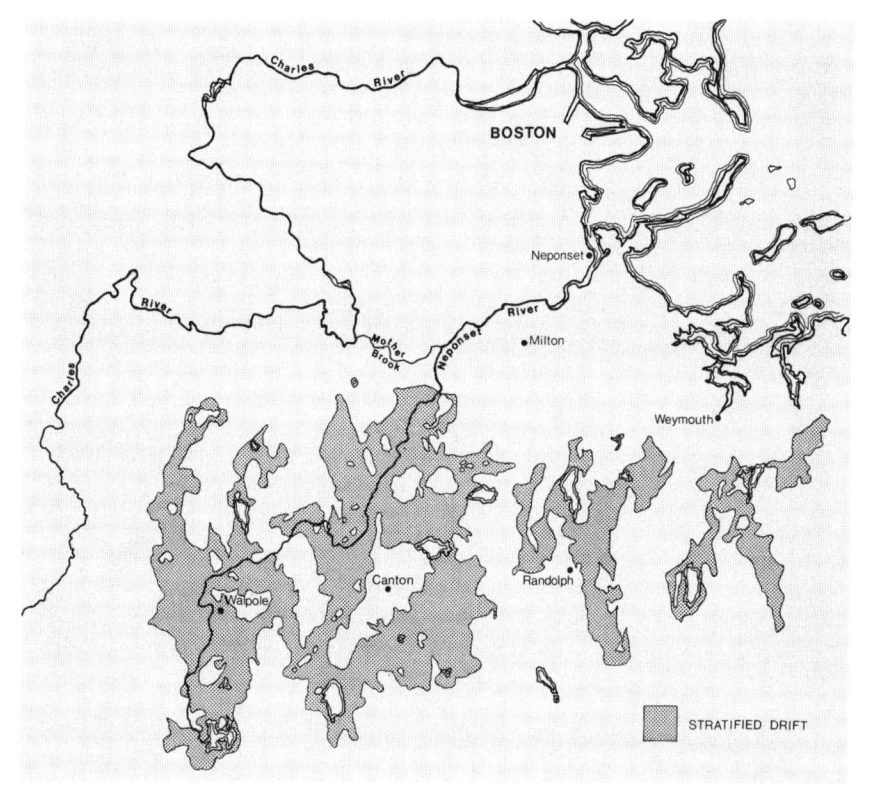

Fig. VI-3
Water Resources of the Neponset and Weymouth River Basins

Adapted from: R. A. Brackley et al., "Hydrology and Water Resources of the Neponset and Weymouth River Basin, Massachusetts," United States Geological Survey (Washington, D.C., 1973).

we create a waterproof land surface. We build an all-year-round environment which resembles the frozen ground of late winter when rains rush off the land to create floods.

A recent study by the New England Division of the U.S. Army Corps of Engineers of the effects of intensifying urbanization in the Winchester-Reading-Burlington suburbs showed that the runoff from the land surface there had increased by fifty percent in the thirty years since 1940. The population of those towns grew by 87 percent in the same period. Since the density of settlement and the condition of the land vary so greatly through the Boston BEA an overall estimate for the region carries little meaning, but we should note that our fifty percent population growth since 1920 inevitably speeded the runoff of our rain.

In addition to the rain, the streams, and the ponds, the big water resource of the region lies buried in its deep and extensive beds of sand and gravel which store water like giant sponges. The lakes and ponds are tell-tales for the level of this stored ground water; as you watch a lake go down in the summer drought, you can reason that the water in the much larger nearby beds of sand, gravel, and clay is also being drained away. This ground water is the source we tap with a well, and it is the source that the rivers and brooks depend upon for their summer flow. It is the source we also depend upon to amplify and supply our reservoirs. If the population of a region draws out water from the ground year after year in excess of what it puts back, and if its takings exceed what the rain replenishes, then the brooks and lakes will dry up, the rivers stop flowing, and, as in one case in Texas, the land itself may even sink.

A recent study in the United States Geological Survey *Atlas* for 1973 of the hydrology of the water resources of the Neponset and Weymouth River basins will make this general model clear. In Figure VI-3, the areas in gray are the aquifers (stratified drift), the sand, gravel and clay beds which store the ground water. Neponset, Milton, and Weymouth are on the north, at the top of the map; Walpole, Canton, and Randolph are at the south, or bottom of the map. The Neponset River can be seen running from Walpole (lower left) to Neponset (upper right). The average yearly rainfall in even such a small area varies by as much as 5 percent. It is highest in the urbanized eastern portion which is closest to the sea.

The average amount of rainfall available to the basin is 43.7 inches per year. Of that sum 21.7 inches is now lost through evapotranspiration, leaving a balance of 22 inches for the valley to work with. Currently the rivers carry off about all of it to the Atlantic, but some is being taken out by town wells and then after its use it is shipped via the Metropolitan District Commission sewer system to Nut and Moon Islands in Boston Harbor.

Now imagine the population of this basin growing, and more and more houses, parking lots, factories, and streets being built. The citizens will demand more and more water and the towns will add wells and draw up more and more water from the ground storage sands. The spread of the waterproof surface in turn will reduce the percolation of rainwater back into the ground. The Neponset will become erratic, flooding with quick storm runoffs, and then becoming sluggish as it is fed less water from the ground. As the river lapses into torpor, storm runoff pollution will become an ever greater share of its diet and the citizens will demand that it be cleaned up. Following present practice, more efficient and all-encompassing sewerage will be constructed so that the water of the basin will go via express to Moon Island without lingering in Walpole or Braintree. In time the towns will become big exporters of the local water, the water table will fall, the Neponset will cease to flow more and more days each year, and in time will become a swamp, because it is too shallow to make a decent lake. Add generous doses of highway salt and a lot of industrial chemicals and this little narrative becomes the history of the Charles River Basin and the future for all the rivers within Route 128.

The water history of the center of our metropolis is paved with good intentions. The history opened in 1639 when the Puritans cut the Mother Brook's channel to deliver water from the Charles to the Neponset so that the falls in Dorchester would better support their mills. According to Michael Frimpter, this diversion takes perhaps a quarter or a third of the stream flow of the Charles.

Next the invention and popularity of the flush toilet caused the city fathers of Boston to change their old rule which forbade the emptying of fecal matter into sewers, and instead they allowed such discharges. From that year on rainwater runoff became polluted runoff.

The rapid growth of the city of Boston and its immediate suburbs in time taxed the capacities of private wells and the city began its drawing of fresh water from outside the Charles River Basin. First, in 1848, it reached into the Merrimack Valley to Lake Cochituate, then to Lake Wachusett, and finally out of the Merrimack to the Connecticut Valley for the Quabbin Reservoir (completed in 1939). Meanwhile population growth brought the outward spread of pollution. At first inner suburbs, like Brookline, had to abandon their wells next to the Charles; then an outer tier like Newton and Waltham; now in recent years, Weston and Wellesley. Similar conditions, and a mistaken pricing policy by the MDC encouraged more and more towns to join the Boston system until now, Frimpter concludes, it serves 34 cities and towns in a band 10 to 15 miles from downtown Boston.

Heavy engineering in water supply necessitated heavy engineering for sewage management. From 1877 to the present Boston and the later MDC constantly enlarged its sewerage lines to carry off the imported water. The target has been to catch up with the outflow of dry-weather sewage. First the strategy was to collect the sewage and pipe it to Boston Harbor, then as this reform shifted the site of pollution to the harbor there have been intermittent improvements to treat the sewage before dumping it into the harbor. The project is not yet complete even in these narrow terms. Sea lettuce multiplies embarrassingly off Winthrop each summer near the Deer Island north sewage outfall. In 1903 the Board of Health first closed the shellfish beds of Boston because of sewage contamination; such incidents have become more frequent over time. Special chlorinators have been installed to handle the storm sewers next to the South Boston beaches, and harbor swimming is often closed altogether. Inland there are still 300,000 people discharging raw sewage (11% of the region's output) into local streams. These problems have been thoroughly documented in a Boston case study by Kennedy Engineers, Inc., and by the Massachusetts Executive Office of Environmental Affairs.

One might view this history with composure, and take hope in the future completion of the metropolitan system and the improvement of its harbor delivery, were it not for the fact that Boston has many rainy days, and that most of the pollution in the inner metropolitan rivers and the harbor comes from the storm runoff water which picks up the other sewage as it floods through the pipes. Since 1945 numerous studies have called for the construction of an elaborate and separate system to handle the rainwater runoff. In 1965 a bold engineer proposed a special deep tunnel system for carrying rain and dry-weather sewage deep underground to a point outside the harbor entirely. The cost was then half a billion dollars. Recently the Environmental Protection Agency and the federal grants-in-aid program have launched projects to divert the storm water and to make the rivers of the BEA swimmable and fishable by 1983. If you look around the city, especially on the banks of the Charles, you can see this work in progress. Unfortunately this massive engineering strategy carries all the signs of turning the inner metropolis into a desert, just as our hypothetical history of the Neponset suggested. Joel A. Tarr and Francis Clay McMichael discuss how one generation's engineering solutions determine the next generation's problems in their study, "Decisions About Wastewater Technology, 1850-1932."

The Charles River now is almost stagnant seven days a year, and if outer suburbs pump more ground water in response to their own population growth, the stagnant times will increase in frequency, according to Frimpter. During the long drought of the sixties water from the Quabbin Reservoir had to be poured into the Charles just to keep it moving! Quabbin itself overran its capacity in 1967 and the MDC is looking to divert more rivers in the Connecticut Valley into its reservoir. Residents there quite logically object to the consequences for themselves.

An alternative strategy to drying out the inner metropolis and then irrigating it with Connecticut River water seems in order. The nineteenth-century, massive engineering strategy seems to have come to a dead end. Many studies are currently underway and alternatives exist. Essentially all call for fragmenting the water and sewer systems of the region into river basins and treating both storm and dry-weather sewage so thoroughly that the water we use can be returned to the groundwater storage beds for lakes, ponds, stream flow, and re-use by citydwellers. These alternative approaches may or may not cost less to install than our old ways. Such systems are currently the methods of Long Island, New York. In any event they seem to more closely approach a goal of living with the rest of nature and fostering a variety of metropolitan ecologies than the export path followed heretofore.

In the management of land all metropolitan conflicts we have touched upon heretofore converge at the local level and become the emotional politics of zoning battles, highway and subdivision hearings, and open-space campaigns. Feelings about a proper family style have been used to zone out communes and even recently to exclude an abortion clinic from one town. The income distribution and racial employment practices of our economy are reflected in local zoning laws which in practice exclude the poor and many persons of color from our towns. Our automobile habits and land exploitation practices can be seen in the air, or read in the rivers and ponds. Finally, our peculiar historic pathwork of taxes and public accounts finds itself endlessly repeated in an absurd logic which passes for practical wisdom among us. A typical statement generally goes: "We must be practical, we cannot afford everything. We cannot afford housing and parks, we must choose between jobs and cleaning up the environment."

Nothing better illustrates our tradition of dividing man from nature than such foolishness. I trust by now, after you have followed me through the many examples from our human settlement and its environment, that I have convinced you that what we cannot afford any longer is this division in our thinking and our policies. The best solutions to our metropolitan problems, and also the cheapest, will be found by merging jobs with the environment, housing with open space, human variety with all other variety, natural man with nature.

The current condition of metropolitan land is a result of a highly detailed and complicated set of historical events. Many strands of history converge to form a particular pattern of built and open space even in one city or town. We do not have time in this lecture, nor has my research come far enough to carry on a discussion at this detailed level.

By way of conclusion, however, I can use a part of my beginning research to tie together for you some of the issues of the way we think about ourselves and about nature with the problems of land management.

Since 1920 our attitudes toward land have been revolutionized. Formerly, except in our largest cities, landowners were free to buy and sell, and to use their property in most any way they chose. Now almost all the land in the Boston BEA has been politicized. We have at last, in what Fred Basselman and David Callies call the "quiet revolution in land," come to think of our land as a limited urban resource in which private decision-making must be subject to public limitation. In short we have politicized something which had formerly been privatized.

To record the progress of this revolution in thought and practice I have been carrying on a study of the spread of zoning legislation throughout the BEA. I have completed the dating of zoning adoptions for Massachusetts and Rhode Island and have gathered a good deal of data on New Hampshire. I have as well plotted the participation of Massachusetts cities and towns in a state program for the acquisition of public open space. This research offers a history of the spread of the new public consciousness of land as an urban resource and also helps to identify some of the conflicts which our current land practices encompass.

It is clear at the outset that government structure is not a significant problem although we often think of our urban problems as being the consequence of inappropriate government organization. Instead, as the Boston metropolis has spread outwards since 1920 our historical structure of state and local government has come more and more to approximate our needs. Three governments, the states of Massachusetts, Rhode Island, and New Hampshire, govern the Boston metropolis. Surely the coordination of three bureaucracies is not an insurmountable obstacle to management of the whole region. Our land problems lie not in government structure, but in divided and confused motives.

Consider for a moment the history of the zoning of land. Today it is an almost universal tool of land management in Massachusetts, and in the Boston BEA as a whole. Zoning gets its name from a mapping process whereby the uses to which land may be put are categorized into zones—residence zones, commercial zones, industrial zones, farming zones, and so forth. The map is prepared by a local planning board and, after hearings and adjustments, a local zoning ordinance sets forth that hereafter all new building must conform to the zones of land uses which appear on the map. Only houses may be built in the residential zone, stores in the commercial zone, etc., etc. Over the years since zoning was introduced its regulations have been much refined and elaborated. Mixed zones for stores and multifamily residences have been popular; industry and commerce intermingled. Class zoning, setting minimum sizes for houses and minimum sizes for lots, as in one- and two-acre lots, has become increasingly popular as a device to see that *our* kind of people continue to dominate an area, instead of *their* kind of people.

As Seymour I. Toll shows in *The Zoned American*, zoning has always reflected conflicts in our popular values and the social turmoil of our cities. The first zoning laws in the nation, in California and New York, had racial and ethnic roots. In California the pioneer law undertook to keep the Chinese out of what were then called "American" neighborhoods; in New York City the first ordinance attempted to stop Jewish garment plants from encroaching on the fashionable shops of Fifth Avenue.

Here in Massachusetts a reasonable desire to render public services more cheaply and efficiently merged with class attitudes about what was and what was not a fitting townscape for a decent family life. The municipal efficiency movement surfaced first, since popular prejudices were already embodied in private convenants between buyers and sellers about the future use of land. In looking at the maps of the spread of zoning it is essential that you realize that until after World War II not only did real-estate dealers and private parties not sell property in some parts of the metropolis to Jews and blacks, but that these prejudices were even written into the deeds to land. Zoning, by making our prejudices public and open, probably has helped us take steps to counteract them.

In 1891 during the peak of the building boom in the city of Boston's own suburban lands, the city instituted controls over subdivision which required that no streets could be laid out without prior approval by the municipal street commissioners. The goal was to supervise street layout, and to prevent scattered and irregular streets and lots which would later require heavy municipal expense to correct, or to pave and tie into water and sewer lines. Acting on a similar impulse the state in 1913 directed every city and town of more than 10,000 inhabitants to establish a planning board to carry on such activities. Thus planning boards preceded zoning here in Massachusetts, as they did not elsewhere. (See the Massachusetts Department of Community Affairs Study Report, *Enabling Legislation for Planning and Zoning,* and the Rhode Island Development Council publication on *Land Use Controls...* for details.)

Then, following the national trends during the twenties Massachusetts, Rhode Island, and New Hampshire authorized cities and towns to institute zoning if they wished. It was a natural step in the evolution of our laws for the public control of private land.

The subsequent adoption of zoning ordinances in the three states tells several things. First, it plots the rise of public consciousness of the necessity to control the private development of land. And because zoning is a matter for cities and towns, a zoning ordinance tells of a decision by local people to concern themselves with the land in their immediate surroundings. Second, the spread of zoning ordinances can suggest whether this public response is merely a reflection of the pressures of building booms and rapid growth, as in the case of Boston, or whether other issues are at stake. If one notices that the first zoning adoptions are limited to the big cities and the fastest growing towns, then municipal efficiency and municipal service problems are perhaps the cause of enactment. If, however, some towns adopt zoning without heavy pressure of building, then perhaps issues of townscape and class are at work. Finally, by comparing the zoning adoptions to recent participation in the state open-space land acquisition program we can sense something about the endurance of traditions of land management within particular cities and towns.

When one compares the rate of population growth in the Boston BEA with the zoning adoptions, the issues of municipal efficiency clearly emerge as the dominant motive for instituting zoning during the years prior to World War II. The population shift map in Chapter I above for 1920-30 (Fig. I-8) shows that the pressure of building was then powerful only in Middlesex, Norfolk, and Providence counties. The largest cities of the region, however, led in zoning adoptions, growing ones like Boston and Providence, as well as depressed ones like New Bedford and Manchester, New Hampshire. Clearly the attempt of these cities was to halt past building abuses which were well known to cities. In those days orderly zoned development was hailed as a way of reducing the costs of municipal street, water, sewer, and utility construction.

There were also in this first decade some interesting anomalies. At the edge of the metropolis, far from the main growth paths, Petersham, Falmouth, and Barnstable initiated zoning. These towns' actions seem to me to be a sign of what we might call townscape politics. The mobilizing of the local government to protect or achieve a particular style of landscape, presumably some preservation of the old town center by controlling industrial and commercial development, and the protection of fringe open lands in large holdings against encroachment by small-lot subdivision. The details of this townscape politics and its variety need further investigation, but the fact that outer suburbs around Boston also adopted zoning in the twenties before heavy development pressure suggests a significant movement among our most affluent towns: Bedford, Concord, Lincoln, Weston, Walpole, and Marshfield. All in this list were towns with large private estates. Such outlying towns and suburbs probably had influential citizens who were very concerned with land planning and conservation, perhaps a concern like that famous estate owner of the era, Franklin Delano Roosevelt.

Population shifts during the Great Depression (Fig. I-9) were at such a low level that no city or town could have adopted zoning in response to building pressure. The motives must have been more prospective. More cities joined the zoning list in these years: Newburyport, Peabody, Leominster, Concord and Portsmouth, New Hampshire. The wealthy fringe was also active: Andover, Carlisle, and Dover.

From 1940 to 1950 Norfolk County grew the most of any in the BEA, and to a lesser degree Plymouth and Middlesex Counties shared the postwar resumption of suburbanization. Most of the zoning action, however, took place to the north of Boston and at other scattered locations like Sekonk, a suburb of Providence, Dunstable and Southbridge, Massachusetts, and Amherst, Canterbury, and New London, New Hampshire. The adoptions look more like the outward diffusion of an idea, than an immediate response to land pressures. It would be possible, however, to think of the adoptions on the South Shore, the string of towns from Hingham to Sharon, and the Cape adoptions of Bourne and Yarmouth, as being triggered by new subdivisions of land.

During the great suburban boom of the sixties, Middlesex and Norfolk counties were already zoned so that population pressure could not reflect itself in adoptions. Instead, the special characteristic of this decade is the extreme reluctance of the towns of Plymouth County to take up zoning, and the spread of zoning outwards through Worcester County, Massachusetts, all of Rhode Island, and into southern New Hampshire.

Since 1960 zoning has become almost universal within a fifty-mile radius of Boston, and is slowly spreading to the outer edges of the BEA.

The spread of zoning in the metropolis seems, thus, to embody three themes: a theme of municipal efficiency in which cities like Boston, Providence, and Manchester took the lead; a theme of townscape planning and class attitudes towards land in which the towns of estate owners took the lead; and a theme of the defense of old-fashioned privatism in which the towns of Plymouth County and other fringe small towns resisted for a long time the relentless logic of a metropolitan human settlement.

A review of the recent experience of Massachusetts with open-land acquisition confirms this zoning history and suggests that we would all profit from a systematic analysis of the varying class attitudes towards land which now exist within the metropolis. The issue is clearly more complex than just exclusionary politics, although the desire to keep poor people and blacks out of towns is a major element in our land behavior. In addition to these negative feelings there seems to be as well a variety of positive goals in the management of land in which we Bostonians differ, as we do in so many things.

In 1961 Massachusetts enacted a Self-Help Land Acquisition Program in which towns wishing to purchase private land for public open space would be assisted by state funds to match the towns' own appropriations. The motive of the legislation was to encourage the creation of open space near where people lived, not in isolated state parks, as had been the former state policy. From 1961 through 1975, according to the Massachusetts Association of Conservation Commissions, 17,405 acres of land have been purchased by cities and towns in 121 separate projects.

The towns which have been most active and ambitious in using this program are the old estate towns which formerly took the lead in suburban zoning: Lincoln, Carlisle, Andover, Concord, Marshfield, and Barnstable. Today these places not only look different than other Boston residential suburbs or fringe mill towns, they also seem to be towns with a history of a distinct kind of land politics. The presence of this group suggests to me that if we looked with similar care at other suburbs and fringe mill towns in the metropolis we would find that there are perhaps five or six different townscapes each with its own characteristic land politics. We should examine this variety because its presence among us can give us a good sense of the range of possibilities we could work with in building a more human metropolitan settlement for ourselves.

When a Massachusetts legislator recently learned that some of the wealthiest towns in the Commonwealth were taking up more of the self-help, open-space funds than the poorer cities, he moved to stop the program. A foolish misapplication of the principle of equity. Our quarrel with these towns is not the beauty and distinctiveness of their land planning, rather it is that they do not pay their just share of the taxes, and that they are beneficiaries of our foolish income distribution customs. Surely it would have been more appropriate for the legislator to have devoted himself to these issues, not to preventing other towns that wished to build a network of beautiful parks such as now exists in Lincoln.

For myself, I draw several conclusions from this brief history of town activism in the management of land. First, consciousness of the necessity for land management in the Boston BEA is now almost universal. Second, this universality of ordinances makes state legislation to set racial, class, and environmental minima both imperative and workable. Third, and finally, in our behavior in the past we can see that no consensus exists among us about the details of town design and environmental management. It is a welcome history, and we should apply to our townscapes that same principle of variety which we seek to amplify in the nonhuman environments we must tend.

VII.

The Symbolic Climate

The subjects of water, air, and land possess a seeming concreteness. They can be measured exactly as gallons, cubic meters, and acres. All are objects of specific laws and public policy, and there is even some regular recording of the outcomes of these regulations and projects. All can be seen as nuts-and-bolts issues, matters which can safely be left to the accumulated wisdom and technique of professional engineers, biologists, and lawyers.

Yet as we explored these subjects from a metropolitan and historical point of view this comforting exactitude melted away. Instead we faced, as in so many aspects of our human settlement, the convergence of disparate lines of historical events, the unwonted appearance of unexpected outcomes, and the multiplication of present problems from past values and attitudes. Whether we looked at the expanding core metropolitan desert, the conflicts over the decontamination of the air, or the patterns of zoning, each subject presented us with the necessity to make choices, to determine for ourselves our metropolitan natural community. No longer can we depend upon a balancing force of outside nature which would protect us from our own folly. And as far as the immediate issues of politics were concerned, amidst this necessity for choice stood the obdurate fact that all the alternatives would be costly, costly both in money and in social change away from our present way of life in metropolitan Boston.

My personal opinion is that the rewards of seeking greater public health, greater natural variety, and greater social equity will be very large, far larger than the costs of change, or the costs of persisting in our present paths. But this is only an opinion of mine which many do not share. For those who see in our water, air, and land problems only added costs, not benefits, the pains of our current metropolitan predicament must indeed be intense. For such people the future of metropolitan life will offer only the excitements of a succession of urban crises.

All the difficulties of knowledge and choice which characterize the natural environment also pervade the subject of our metropolitan symbolic climate, and they do so at a much higher intensity of ignorance, uncertainty, and conflict of goals. Those dimensions of the symbolic climate which can be measured easily—the number, origin, and destination of letters and telephone calls, the listenership of radio and television stations, the readership of newspapers and magazines, and the sales of books—such dimensions lack a convincing theory to give them meanings as determinants of modern life in an American metropolis. That which cannot be measured easily—the content and impact of all the letters, telephone calls, radio and television programs, newspapers, magazines, and books—is the subject of the widest speculation, a speculation which runs from self-serving justification of present conditions, to predictions of the dawning of a new era of world peace and harmony, or alternatives of world destruction.

For myself, I cannot come before you as an expert. The network of communications has not been in the past a coin traded among urban historians. The specific field of knowledge in question is quite new to me, and I can only report to you what any intelligent reader might find in some of the most available materials. I can, however, say with a confidence growing out of twenty years as an urban historian, that no subject is more important for an appreciation of urban life than communications. Communications are the essence of cities. We have noted the effect of changes in communications upon the pattern of human settlement here in Boston, in the cycle of nineteenth-century concentration and the counter cycle of twentieth-century diffusion. Whether you want to understand what it is like to live in Boston today, or what it was like in Boston in 1870, or to guess what Boston might be in the year 2000, you must think about the way we communicate with each other.

Because of my ignorance, and also because of what I perceive to be the confusion of the subject itself, I shall refrain from commenting upon public policy, as I sometimes have in discussing other aspects of our metropolitan life. Let me only call to your attention the very special public-policy situation which prevails here in the United States.

Throughout most of the world communications are tightly controlled by governments. The governors of most of mankind consider open communications to be too dangerous to political stability to be allowed to flow as freely as they do here in the United States. Surely we can take this fact as further evidence that we are touching upon a topic of some importance in the life of a human settlement.

The first amendment to the federal Constitution and the constitutions of all the states set forth a common goal for a communications policy: government should not censor, and therefore by implication, should not impede the free flow of messages among its citizens. Neither local, state, nor federal governments have, however, been able completely to privatize communications. The physics of space and electronics compel public intervention because it creates natural monopolies which themselves restrict communications. The natural monopolies of space call forth sign ordinances from cities and towns, and local and state governments have yet to find a comfortable balance between the desirability of untrammeled expression and the perceived social damage of false advertising, inflammatory statements, and some kinds of religious and sexual statements. Television, radio, telephone, and telegraph are all subject to federal regulation, the mails are a federal monopoly, and all levels of government arrange among themselves to tap telephones, and open telegrams and mail, and, under what are called "emergency conditions," all practice censorship of the press and electronic media.

The conflict between private rights and public demands was not ended by the founding fathers, but they set the terms of the argument. If you go to your library shelf you will find most of the American books on communications concern themselves with one or another aspect of private freedom of expression. Many commentators (David Halberstam, for example, in the *Atlantic*) argue that despite our favorable situation we are still very far from the maximum openness which could be achieved even in the face of the natural monopolies which modern communications create.

The most interesting literature, however, does not restrict itself to the narrow compass of constitutional implications and industry regulation. Instead it views the totality of modern metropolitan life, and places communications in the context of society as a whole. Since such a view is very much our goal in considering the recent history of Boston, this approach offers us the greatest rewards. The fact that the writing is often apocalyptic only makes it even more suitable to our local taste for guilt and punishment.

This school of thought focusses on a central paradox of modern metropolitan life. On the one side stand the undoubted wealth of all levels of society and the extraordinary multiplication of modes of communication. On the opposite side stand three distinct but interwoven kinds of impoverishment. First, the impoverishment of the human mind and spirit through the narrowing of the range of ideas and alternatives which artists, scientists, and scholars are willing to contemplate and to investigate. Second, the impoverishment of commonplace understanding and feeling through the dominance of formal and mechanical modes of communication in everyday living. Third, the impoverishment of most people's sense of mastery and self-esteem through their growing powerlessness in jobs, politics, and social organizations of all kinds.

The argument is complex and picks up many historical threads. Let us begin with an early and relatively simple model of the direction of change in modern society—E. M. Forster's short story, "The Machine Stops."

The story, published in 1909, has its roots in the late-nineteenth-century urban-industrial crises when both English and American thinkers, appalled by the contradictions of mechanized cities and their mass poverty, lost their faith in the current path of history which until then had been widely thought to have been benign and progressive. One group saw the possibility for relief from such intolerable conditions in the exploration of technological Utopias. Our local novelist of this school was Edward Bellamy whose *Looking Backward* (1888), a Utopia for Boston, attracted world-wide attention, and even spawned a minor political movement which in turn contributed to Ebenezer Howard's thinking in *Garden Cities of To-morrow* and to the later rise of the new-town school of urban planning.

Forster, himself, was responding to the Utopias

proposed by H. G. Wells's science fiction. Forster's line of attack challenges the reasoning of Utopians and their contemporaries who sought ever more elaborated technological solutions for problems which had been created by technology in the first place.

The story is set in a future age which has abolished poverty by a retreat into a vast underground mechanized beehive. People are secure there against the elements, and every material need is provided to the cell-dwellers by means of a highly elaborated and hierarchically organized set of machines. Forster begins:

> Imagine, if you can, a small room, hexagonal in shape, like the cell of a bee. It is lighted neither by window nor by lamp, yet it is filled with radiance. There are no apertures for ventilation, yet the air is still fresh. There are no musical instruments, and yet, at the moment that my meditation opens, this room is throbbing with melodious sounds. An arm-chair is in the center, by its side is a reading desk—that is all the furniture. And in the arm-chair there sits a swaddled lump of flesh—a woman, about five feet high, with a face as white as a fungus. It is to her the little room belongs. (*Collected Tales*, p. 144)

> There were buttons and switches everywhere —buttons to call for food, for music, for clothing. There was the hot-bath button, by pressure of which a basin of (imitation) marble rose out of the floor, filled to the brim with a warm deodorized liquid. There was the cold-bath button. There was the button that produced literature. And there were of course the buttons by which she communicated with her friends. The room, although it contained nothing, was in touch with all that she cared for in the world. (pp. 149-50)

The essence of life in this world was communication. Not direct communication, people never gathered together, they never touched each other, but electronic communications for music, films, and lectures. In response to these stimuli individuals talked to each other through videophones about their reactions to the public lectures and entertainments they alternately watched or gave to each other.

The first interruption in the equilibrium of the heroine—a mother, Vashti—came when her son made a novel, but not illegal, communications demand. He asked his mother to come to visit him so that they could speak together face to face.

> "I have called you before, mother, but you were always busy or isolated. I have something particular to say."
> "What is it dearest boy? Be quick. Why could you not send it by pneumatic post?"
> "Because I prefer saying such a thing. I want———"
> "Well?"
> "I want you to come and see me."
> Vashti watched his face in the blue plate.
> "But I can see you!" she exclaimed. "What more do you want?"
> "I want to see you not through the Machine," said Kuno (her son). "I want to speak to you not through the wearisome Machine."
> "Oh, hush!" said his mother, vaguely shocked. "You mustn't say anything against the Machine."
> "Why not?"
> "One mustn't."
> "You talk as if a god had made the Machine," cried the other. "I believe that you pray to it when you are unhappy. Men made it, do not forget that. Great men, but men. The Machine is much, but it is not everything. I see something like you in this plate, but I do not see you. I hear something like you through this telephone, but I do not hear you. That is why I want you to come. Come stop with me. Pay me a visit, so that we can meet face to face, and talk about the hopes that are in my mind." (pp. 146-47)

Vashti does go by airship to visit her son. The trip is very unpleasant for her because so much is strange and unfamiliar. Kuno lives in a distant cell in the northern hemisphere. He tells his mother of his brief escape from the underground living machine to the surface of the earth. There he sees the stars and wild nature, and even catches a glimpse of a few humans who have escaped the machine and live on the earth as men did centuries ago. In Kuno's telling of his physical preparations for the task of exploration beyond the machine he proposes a classical test for high-technology impoverishment.

> "You know that we have lost the sense of space. We say 'space is annihilated,' but we have annihilated not space, but our sense thereof. We have lost a part of ourselves. I determined to recover it, and I began by walking up and down the platform of the railway outside my room. Up and down, until I was tired, and so did recapture the meaning of 'Near' and 'Far.' 'Near' is a place to which I can get quickly *on my feet*, not a place to which the train or the air-ship will take me

quickly. 'Far' is a place to which I cannot get quickly on my feet; the vomitory [the orifice through which the airships enter and leave the underground hive] is 'far,' though I could be there in thirty-eight seconds by summoning the train. Man is the measure. That was my first lesson. Man's feet are the measure for distance, his hands are the measure for ownership, his body is the measure for all that is loveable and desirable and strong." (p. 167)

Kuno is dragged back into the machine by its fixing apparatus and is transferred to a room near his mother. Then slowly the machine begins to break down. The first stage of the breakdown brings political repression to the inhabitants. Everyone is forbidden permission to travel on the surface of the earth, authorizations for explorations are withdrawn. Second, worship of the machine itself is established as a revival of religion among a formerly secular people.

Forster writes at this point about the inevitability of massive disequilibria which must attend any overcentralized organization.

> To attribute these two great developments to the Central Committee, is to take a very narrow view of civilization. The Central Committee announced the developments, it is true, but they were no more the cause of them than were the kings of the imperialistic period the cause of war. Rather did they yield to some invisible pressure, which came no one knew whither, and which, when gratified, was succeeded by some new pressure, equally invisible. To such a state of affairs it is convenient to give the name of progress. No one confessed that the Machine was out of hand. Year by year it was served with increasing efficiency and decreased intelligence. The better a man knew his own duties upon it, the less he understood the duties of his neighbor, and in all the world there was no one who understood the monster as a whole. Those master brains had perished. They had left full directions, it is true, and their successors have mastered a portion of those directions. But Humanity, in its desire for comfort, had overreached itself. It had exploited the riches of nature too far. Quietly and complacently, it was sinking into decadence, and progress had come to mean the progress of the Machine. (pp. 185-86)

The story ends with the collapse of the machine and the death of all its inhabitants. Vashti and Kuno die together, their fear and pain relieved by the knowledge that human life still existed among the few refugees on the surface of the earth, and that man would survive despite the destruction of most of the world's population.

In Forster's story we meet a very common way of thinking about our modern metropolitan life. The vast scale and complexity of the metropolis which multiplies a narrowness of thought and a rigidity in much of our everyday social interactions suggest a giant machine and mechanical parts. By contrast, the seeming simplicity, flexibility, and playfulness of an individual person suggest that man might well be the opposite to our cities and therefore a more appropriate measure for our social arrangements.

However popular and sensible these metaphorical opposites may seem, they are nevertheless insufficient. Although telephone operators and some factory and office workers whose labor is paced by machines suffer directly from dominance by machines, most of us do not. Rather it is the rigidity and inhumanity of our fellow humans which confronts us and is the principle source of our complaints.

In recent years a number of stereotypes have come forward to express the quality of human interactions in the American metropolis—the man in the gray flannel suit, the man in uniform, the plastic woman. What we are recording by such labels is our sense that some inherent, some natural humanity fails to break free from the formal roles of the company or government bureaucrat, the policeman or soldier, the saleswoman or airline stewardess. The petty and gross tyrannies which people promulgate from such roles suggest that we must be careful in defining just what it is about man which is to be the measure of our human society.

The essence of the attack on long-range trends in modern society rests on the observation that large-scale human organizations through their definition and control over people's roles are responsible for the inhumanity of our human settlement. The leading author of this school is Lewis Mumford who recently summarized his writing on modern culture and cities in his *Pentagon of Power* (1970). Mumford places symbols and communications in the context of the modern unleashing of the age-old human appetite for domination and control of others. His argument is complex, and spans four centuries, but for our purposes it should suffice to notice how he treats the human consequences of large-scale modern institutions, and where he places modern modes of communications in the organization of power.

In Mumford's view science and technology, because they are narrowly directed at what is immediately profitable and at what will augment the power of the state and other corporate bodies, simultaneously multiply the number of mechanized products for human consumption, and multiply the mechanized products of warfare. Because income redistribution does not generally benefit governments but rather threatens the state with conflict and turmoil, such redistribution is rarely attempted. Instead, traditional hierarchies of power and reward are preserved and elaborated so that much of the population gains a personal sense of lifetime material progress. We noted this phenomenon in our review of three possible scenarios for average Boston families since 1920. We noted too that the national demand for armaments had assisted our metropolis in its transition from an early textile industrialization to a modern electronics one.

The benefits of a society arranged according to such principles are clear enough: prosperity for all, and relief from the most arduous forms of physical and clerical labor. On the job, the work setting becomes more sociable and relaxed as tasks grow easier. But simultaneous with this gain, most employees become more and more powerless to control their tasks, to fashion their product, to repair the machines they use, or to define legitimate goals for themselves other than those which magnify the organization. Much of what we do in our offices which is humane, and for which we justly take pride, is against the rules, or is a manipulation of the rule book. As a result work among us becomes easier and more chatty than it was fifty years ago, but the range of intellectual and emotional rewards from work becomes steadily narrowed. From these historical trends sprang the gray flannel man and the plastic woman.

Perhaps such an all-encompassing history seems too grand to you; something that exceeds the boundaries necessary to a consideration of fifty years of social trends in one provincial American metropolis. Let me make a direct connection for you between Mumford and your Boston by reading to you a passage from an author who lives among us and knows us very well—John Updike. In his novel, *Couples* (1968), he speaks about the thrust of suburban and downtown life here in Boston during the 1950's.

> The Applebys and the Little-Smiths had moved to Tarbox in the middle Fifties, unknown to each other, though both men worked in securities on State Street, Harold as a broker, Frank as a trust officer in a bank. Frank had gone to Harvard, Harold to Princeton. They belonged to that segment of their generation of the upper middle class which mildly rebelled against the confinement and discipline whereby wealth maintained its manners during the upheavals of depression and world war. Raised secure amid national trials and introduced as adults into an indulgent economy, into a business atmosphere strangely blended of crisp youthful energy and underlying depersonalization, of successful small-scale gambles carried out against a background of rampant diversification and the ultimate influence of a government whose taxes and commissions and appetites for armaments set limits everywhere, introduced into a nation whose leadership allowed a toothless moralism to dissemble a certain practiced cunning, into a culture whose adolescent passions and homosexual philosophies were not yet triumphant, a climate still *furtively* hedonist, of a country still too overtly threatened from without to be ruthlessly self-abusive, a climate of in-between, of stand-off, and day-by-day, wherein all generalizations, even negative ones, seemed unintelligent—to this new world the Applebys and the Little-Smiths brought a modest determination to be free, to be flexible, and to be decent. (pp. 105-6)

I read Updike's book, *Couples*, to be a series of stories about the inevitable failure of middle-class suburban life to support all the demands which its men and women placed upon it.

These limitations of families are fully appreciated among us today here in Boston, and like our parents we often turn to the media for escape or enlargement of our lives. In 1920 newspapers, magazines, and books were the popular home connections to the pipelines of commercial news and fantasy. Soon thereafter radio, and since World War II television, became the dominant mass media. What Bostonians and other Americans have faced when they turned to receive these communications will be the task of our speculations for the balance of these lectures. We will concentrate on fiction because here, surely, we should find the freest play of the imagination and therefore the fullest offerings of supplements to what was missing in ordinary people's workaday metropolitan lives. Let us begin with a best-seller of the twenties, a book which is also regarded as a masterpiece of our literature.

F. Scott Fitzgerald's, *The Great Gatsby* (1925), is a novel of power, mindless, unbridled power. As a portrait of twentieth-century American metropolitan life it fits exactly into Mumford's analysis that the lack of humane goals for the exercise of power is at the root of our current problems. We can see in the novel too, a partial answer to our earlier economic riddle of why the multiplication of thousands of individual decisions, each beneficial to the person making them, often added up to social destruction.

Published in 1925 Fitzgerald's book has long been accepted as an accurate portrait of the trends of our times. Its main figure, Jay Gatsby, is a romantic hero, a man of large deeds and great visions, who, unlike the rest of us, makes no small plans, but does everything on a grandiose scale. His wealth is incalculable, his summer house gigantic, his cars, clothes, and parties fabulous. People flock towards him because his lavish expenditures, so carelessly made, radiate the energy of power which always draws those who are enmeshed in the ordinary fears and small successes and failures of commonplace life. We marvel at those who rise above us, and hope that by standing near them some of the excess of their triumph will fall to ourselves. The imperial Presidency of our own time is a political exploitation of this common human reaction.

The specifics of Gatsby's life, and the nature of his heroism, are thought by literary critics to be a profound comment on the state of modern America. Marius Bewley, for example, in an article on Fitzgerald's criticism of America, in the *Sewanee Review*, suggests that the hero's life fits the conventions of American morality in uncomfortable ways. A poor boy, the son of an unsuccessful midwestern farmer, Gatsby tried working his way through a small denominational college, but dropped out and bummed around at odd jobs as so many young people do. All the while he dreamed that someday he would make his fortune, become a somebody. Surely here is an appropriate and admirable beginning for an American life. Gatsby even kept a list of resolutions for himself, as Benjamin Franklin had advised. (pp. 152-3)

Rise from bed	6.00 A.M.
Dumbell exercise & wall scaling	6.15-6.30 A.M.
Study electricity, etc.	7.15-8.15 A.M.
Work	8.30-4.30 P.M.
Baseball and sports	4.30-5.00 P.M.
Practice elocution, poise and how to attain it	5.00-6.00 P.M.
Study needed inventions	7.00-9.00 P.M.

GENERAL RESOLVES

No wasting time at Shafters or [name unintelligible]
No more smoking or chewing
Bath every other day
Read one improving book or magazine per week
Save $5.00 [crossed out] $3.00 per week
Be better to parents

His opportunity to learn about the big world of money and power came from the sponsorship of an older man—an almost universal pattern for every rising young man in our city today. But Gatsby's training was unusual. His sponsor was a drunken and worn-out old man, Dan Cody, an exploiter of man and nature, a victor in the struggles for control of the vast copper ores of Montana, and a winner in many gold and silver strikes elsewhere. Gatsby, as a servant on Cody's wandering yacht, learns about the world. He is a hero, however, and is not corrupted, as you or I might be, by such tawdry circumstances. He continues to dream of greatness.

Some years later, and after a very successful term of service in World War I, he makes a large fortune

—as a bootlegger, a partner of gamblers, and an investor in all manner of shady schemes. When we first meet him through the accident of his house being next to the cottage of our narrator (a neophyte bond broker just come from the midwest), he remains uncorrupted by his dealings and acquaintances. He is still very much the romantic hero, a man of pure heart, enormous power and energy, and fabulous dreams. Fitzgerald, by keeping Gatsby, as opposed to the lesser characters, in a soft focus, means us to understand that Gatsby is, in the summer of 1922, the modern embodiment of an American hero.

In a famous passage at the end of the book Fitzgerald tells us how we should see his novel, in case we missed the point along the way.

> Most of the big shore places were closed now and there were hardly any lights except the shadowy, moving glow of a ferryboat across the Sound. And as the moon rose higher the inessential houses began to melt away until gradually I became aware of the old island here that flowered once for Dutch sailors' eyes—a fresh, green breast of the new world. Its vanished trees, the trees that had made way for Gatsby's house, had once pandered in whispers to the last and the greatest of all human dreams; for a transitory enchanted moment man must have held his breath in the presence of this continent, compelled into an aesthetic contemplation he neither understood nor desired, face to face for the last time in history with something commensurate with his capacity for wonder. (pp. 158-159)

"America the last and greatest of all human dreams . . . the wonder of a new continent. . . . Compelled into an aesthetic contemplation he neither understood or desired. . . ." the vastness, complexity, and beauty of wild nature. Such feelings can take one towards thoughts of God or Eden, or both, depending upon one's emotional life.

And what does the American hero do when presented with such a last chance? He shoots it, burns it, conquers it, drives mines, plants farms, and runs up cities.

By Fitzgerald's time this continental exhibition of power had shifted its subjects and locations from the wilderness and the west, to money and cities. Thus the Prohibition bonanza and a bootlegger are fitting additions to that long line of callous American power figures—the slash-and-burn pioneer, the slave owner, the factory builder, the whale hunters, and the China merchants. Altogether Fitzgerald's hero makes a formidable indictment of American society. He builds his case on the observation that we have repeatedly failed to harness the energy and wealth of our people and our continent for humane purposes.

Gatsby is brought down, indeed murdered, because he harbors a modern and almost universal American version of the Eden dream. This driver and despoiler of men, for that is after all the business of a bootlegger, has his other side, what is popularly called the "softer side." It appears in his longings for peace, acceptance, and tranquility. Characteristically American too, Gatsby's Eden is no urban commune or Utopian farm settlement in Indiana, but is a search for a secure social triumph. His Eden is a beautiful rich girl, Daisy Buchanan, and in Gatsby's fantasy together they will build a secure and timeless bower. Perhaps you've seen some movies with this theme?

In telling his story Fitzgerald does not, like your lecturer, give you a lot of social history about the overburdening of the American family, but relentlessly drives towards his main theme of the bankruptcy of a society built upon the celebration of power.

What could have been more commonplace and laudable in our American terms than a young man, a promising Army officer, dating a wealthy girl, and dreaming of coming home to marry her? Isn't social mobility one of the tasks to which every American and Boston family is supposed to bend? And what could be more natural in these circumstances than a young man's projecting upon that plastic object, the debutante, his dreams for personal triumph and happiness? Only because Gatsby is raised to the level of a romantic hero who will not give up his youthful dreams, does he direct his whole life towards achieving at any cost what he does not yet possess.

Fitzgerald is relentless, too, in exposing the emptiness of this cluster of American values. As one ascends the social ladder, graded as it is by money, the increase in power only increases the families' possibilities for evil. The Buchanans have a successful marriage. They stay together, and they share an agreement to tolerate, if not encourage, each other's self-aggrandizement. They are people of established wealth, aged money, daughter and son of fortunes made in manufacturing, banking, or railroads a generation before Gatsby. Daisy seeks self-expression in the world of society glamor and entertainment; Tom leads a restless life flexing his muscles and money in polo and a succession of mistresses. Daisy is a hit-and-run driver who kills a pedestrian; Tom is an accessory to a murder. Both kill people because it is easier for them to kill than to take responsibility for their own lives and actions, and because they are so rich they can live that way.

Nick Carraway, the young bond salesman from the midwest who tells the tale, clinches the story by tying up all the threads of Fitzgerald's argument. It is through Nick's eyes that we see Gatsby and the Buchanans, and therefore it is worth inquiring where Mr. Carraway stands.

Nick represents such a socialized equilibrium of power as our nation enjoys. He is a young Yale man, a veteran, who comes from Minnesota to New York to try his fortune in a fashionable, but eminently respectable line of work. We are asked to rest confidence in his judgement for two reasons. First, he is a nice guy, he is what most of us aspire to be, nice guys, people who do not ask too much of themselves, others, or the world. Nick Carraway seems to be the same kind of person thirty years earlier as John Updike's Applebys and Little-Smiths. All are people of moderate education, moderate expectations and moderate wealth. Second, Carraway can be trusted because he has family behind him. For three generations his family has run a successful wholesale hardware business in St. Paul, and at the end of the novel Nick is presumably returning to take his place in this firm. Notice that the wholesale hardware business is an institution of the old economy not the new. He will find a bride from among the local girls who were sent east to boarding-school and college, and presumably will settle down to a comfortable, useful, even civic, suburban life, and will live as happily as Americans can. Nick Carraway's focus is the criticism of old money for new, of settled upper-middle-class family ways towards the ungenteel strivings of immigrants, blacks, and nouveau Americans of all kinds.

In the context of the violence and exploitation of big money in America and New York City in 1922 such social restraint and moderation is surely a virtue. It is the moral platform upon which Fitzgerald built his criticism of our society. But neither Fitzgerald nor his alter ego, Carraway, see alternatives. Their wisdom is to see so clearly that America is a place that worships power, and that such worship is bankrupt and decadent.

I have been to St. Paul, and like New York, it shows the achievements of power and science. Its landscape does not present such dramatic symbols as New York's view from the Queensboro Bridge. Nevertheless, like all American cities, its architecture and engineering tell of the harnessing of a continent and the exploitation of man and nature. St. Paul also has its Valley of Ashes, but on a smaller scale than the dumps Gatsby and the Buchanans go through on their trips between the center of the metropolis and their suburban summer houses. Gatsby and the parents of the Buchanans, however, did not build these cities of power and ashes all by themselves. We the moderate people built them too.

Fitzgerald is very clear on this point. Early in the novel he employs the same sort of vision of the city which he later uses in the vision-of-nature passage at the end of the book. The "white heaps and sugar lumps" of buildings represent the great city's contribution to the beauty of the world, like the trees and "fresh green breast of the new world" on Long Island. Both views inspire feelings of wonder in the beholder. The city vision, however, is marred by the beholder's unease that what he sees is the embodiment of money which smells from exploitation.

> Over the great bridge, with the sunlight through the girders making a constant flicker upon the moving cars, with the city rising up across the river in white heaps and sugar lumps all built with a wish out of non-olfactory money. The city seen from the Queensboro Bridge is always the city seen for the first time, in its first wild promise of all the mystery and the beauty in the world. (p. 63)

Thus Mumford, as a cultural historian looking backwards from 1970, and Fitzgerald, a novelist reporting on the trends of the twenties, both agree that the driving force of modern metropolitan America is power, and that our nation's worship and encouragement of the individual's lust for power are destroying a continent and a people. They, and many of our finest artists and writers, agree that power is the essence of our symbolic climate, and in their works they make this perception available to us all.

But is this the theme that runs through our mass-media presentations? What stories come towards Americans when they pick up a magazine? Could it be that when we turn to find relief from the tensions, inadequacies, and failings of our everyday life we are greeted by heroes and heroines who struggle in such an arena?

Strange and sometimes wonderful things happen in the world of American mass communications. Listen in next time.

VIII.

A Mirror for Strangers

One of the most baffling qualities of the symbolic climate of a modern metropolis is its incessant mixing of old and new ingredients. The action, the plots of both our news and fiction seem terribly old, they repeat endlessly the same few story lines. Newswriters fashion every piece they report into the form of a sporting event, the clash between two opponents: the governor vs. the mayor, Congress vs. the President, Russia vs. the United States, the developers vs. the conservationists, criminals vs. the police, youth vs. the Establishment. The goal is clearly to attract and to hold our attention by offering action where none may be present, or by compressing complicated interactions into an easily comprehensible mold.

In fiction, in make-believe, our taste runs along complementary lines. We like to focus on the hero or heroine and to see the story unfold in terms of the struggle of the individual against an identified enemy: his passion, an adversary, or defined obstacles of society. Many variations are possible within this structure of plot, but the individual compels our attention.

This obsession with paired conflict in news, and with individual plights in fiction seems very traditional and comfortable for those of us who live in America. In fact these are media signs of the very tradition which Fitzgerald, in *The Great Gatsby*, was attacking with his story of a heroic bootlegger and a murderous millionaire couple. They are as well some of the tell-tale marks which Mumford, as a cultural historian, believes reveal a society wedded to a self-destructive worship of power as the ultimate test of personal worth.

The most strident quality of our symbolic climate is not, however, its dependence upon traditional themes. Rather it shouts novelty, irreverence, and iconoclasm. Fashion tumbles upon fashion. Each day's media enthusiasm is puffed as an exciting and progressive leap forward in human living styles. As the old movies repeatedly told us the fox trot was more liberating than the waltz, the twist in turn was an advance in human expression over the fox trot, and now the hustle surely offers an interaction between men and women which none of the foregoing could match. Today lineage and roots are the essence of a sane adjustment to modern life, while yesterday a focus upon youth, and "now," held the best promise for human happiness. The poor among us are alternately discovered and forgotten, blacks come to the fore only to be elbowed aside by white women, and the women are upstaged by the urban descendants of immigrants. Priests marry and lesbians take up childrearing, men and women discover living alone, and love it. The serious goals, the complex social meanings, even the simple pleasures of each fashion are drowned beneath the rushing flood of media output.

The overall consequences for human life within such a dense fog of messages are serious. The rush towards novelty and the multiplicity of one-way communications sources—radio, television, newspapers, theaters, signs, mailings, and advertising of all kinds—produces what communications analysts call *noise*. Noise is a sound without human meaning. We noticed in our discussion of the metropolitan natural environment a recent enthusiasm for wild nature. The rush to the countryside is in part a popular reaction to the high level of metropolitan noise. One has to leave the city and its suburbs to find privacy and intimacy. Personally, I think the fashion to move into old inner-city neighborhoods is also in part motivated by a desire to escape the noise of contemporary commercial media and their symbols.

Cities, however, have always been noisy in just this way—full of hawkers, signs, the clamor of the market, and the pageants and shouting of politics. More serious than the sheer volume and reach of the noise today is the profound confusion which the messages within the noise engender. Whenever one stops to listen to what is being said it is always the same. The outpouring of novelty, the parade of personal and intimate testimony, are cast in a few traditional roles and plots. Although our experience with world wars and decisive changes within the Boston metropolis tells us that powerful historical changes have been taking place in our lifetimes, the media re-run the same show over and over again.

This smog of messages within which we make our urban lives seems nicely adapted to the needs of a commercial system of communications. Incessant novelty suits its competitive demands for readers and listeners. The dynamism of our metropolitan media is the clamor for audiences. The ordering of all facts and all fiction into familiar themes is another crowd-pleaser: one entertains, one diverts, one does not challenge or offend.

I find it hard to suppress the paranoia which such self-evident facts about our symbolic climate encourage. It is not hard to see a conspiracy of the powerful in all of this. The owners of the television, radio, and publishing houses seek to enrich themselves by entertaining us with novelty and by comforting us with repeated reaffirmation of our traditional ways of seeing ourselves. They exclude from our view those facts and modes of thought which suggest that changes should be made in the power relationships of the society.

Herbert I. Schiller in his book *The Mind Managers* takes this point of view. He sees today's metropolitan symbolic climate as being the product of a fusion of government and private corporate interests. His analysis of the media takes him beyond a simple discovery of the military-industrial complex. That power and uniformity of interest does exist; it forced itself upon our attention during the Vietnam War, and it lends a dangerous absurdity to our foreign policy and Defense Department budget debates.

Schiller's interests, however, carry him past these narrow, albeit essential, issues to a more general consideration of how media messages function in modern American society. Two cases he chooses, *T.V. Guide* and the *National Geographic*, carry his argument beyond the realm of direct manipulation of news and fiction. Both magazines employ the standard muddling of novelty and tradition. *T.V. Guide* frequently takes up some timely social conflict, but in fact does no more than touch upon it. It confines its treatment to the recognition of the novelty itself, nothing more. The *National Geographic* trades in information about the exotic, especially distant places and people. These curiosities are treated by the *Geographic* according to the traditional American prejudices about picturesque white natives in costumes, brown natives in pajamas, and black natives with few clothes at all. In the context of all the messages coming towards us, not just the immediately political ones, Schiller sees certain dominant capitalistic and individualistic traditions of our culture coming together with a vigorous pursuit of profit and self-interest. The result is a symbolic climate which steadily narrows our perceptions of the world around us.

Let us pursue the implications of this view of the symbolic climate of our human settlement a little further. Let us take as a case one of the central concerns of this series of lectures. We have noted in several connections that our peculiar system of income and power rewards breeds all manner of social difficulties among those of us who have settled together here in Boston. We have noted as well the increasing corporate organization of our society in government, private business, education, labor, and health. Last lecture we reviewed several summaries of the symbolic climate of the modern urban world and found that a variety of observers saw the corporate organization of power to be the outstanding characteristic of twentieth-century metropolitan living. All this information points towards Schiller's view of the media role.

If these conditions dominate our lives, and if we can find confirmation for this view in the office buildings, factories, and stores, and our daily experience within them, why does this material not appear on the evening television? or in our popular magazines, newspapers, and novels? If this is the essence of our situation, if this is the way we really live, why doesn't this essence pervade our news and fiction?

In point of fact, little appears, and what does appear avoids explorations of power relationships. We have an abundance of certain kinds of business news, and chatty office comedies like the Mary Tyler Moore show, but few stories focus factually, and less still imaginatively, on the power conflicts of such a world. Perhaps what we have been discussing in this lecture series is the object of a taboo, topics forbidden to mass audiences, like sexual intercourse on prime time.

At one level the media certainly does censor out such news and fiction. A standup comic can poke fun at General Motors or the UAW, but an extended questioning treatment is strictly forbidden. Spon-

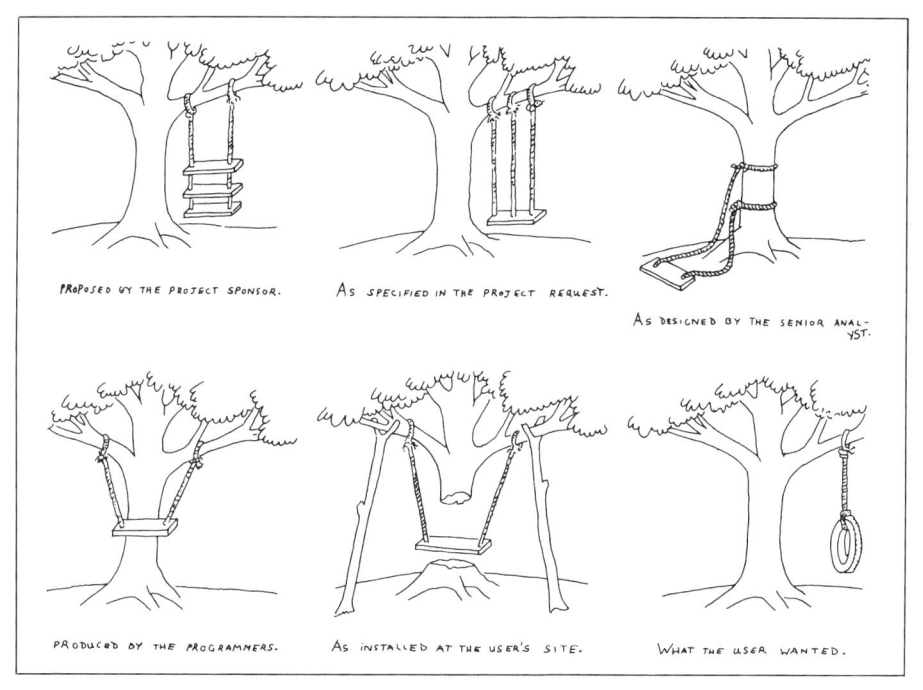

Fig. VIII-1 "Project Swing" I

Source: Allan Dundes and Carl R. Pagter, *Urban Folklore from the Paperwork Empire* (Austin, Texas, 1975). Reproduced by permission of the American Folklore Society from *Urban Folklore from the Paperwork Empire*, American Folklore Society Memoir Series, Vol. 62: 168, 1975. Nor for further reproduction.

sors would not tolerate it, the proprietors fear reprisals, and perhaps as well all the managers of the media are so enmeshed in their corporate world as to be unable to see the desirability for such news or stories.

But censorship alone will not explain our society's feeble production in these topics. Were censorship the only cause of their absence from the media, then one could find a lively underground press and a set of radical authors whose works attracted an eager following. Every revolutionary I have read about tells of reading in his youth advanced or scandalous books—novels by Zola or Dostoyevski, or the works of Marx—and compelled by their power and reasoning the young revolutionary saw his everyday life in a new light.

It is just this reordering of the facts of corporate life we lack, not the facts themselves. True, many private office buildings and factories, many union headquarters and government buildings are protected by guards and security measures which keep all strangers out, but our shortage of inside facts is not our severest lack. If one goes to the radical magazine shelf no exciting underground literature appears—rather the tired reworkings of formulas which were already out of date by World War I.

Perhaps corporate life is a dull subject at best, and does not lend itself to compelling imaginative works. Surely it is not duller than poverty, factories, and mines which for a century provided the central themes for some of our best authors—Dickens, Balzac, Zola, and that stream of American realists which opens with Garland and Howells and floods forward to Dos Passos and Steinbeck.

Perhaps my analysis is all wrong. Contemporary corporate life is so much more prosperous than what preceded it, that its problems must be slight, and my expectation that we should have a literature which reflects its power conflicts is a personal quirk, a product of an iconoclastic professor's mind.

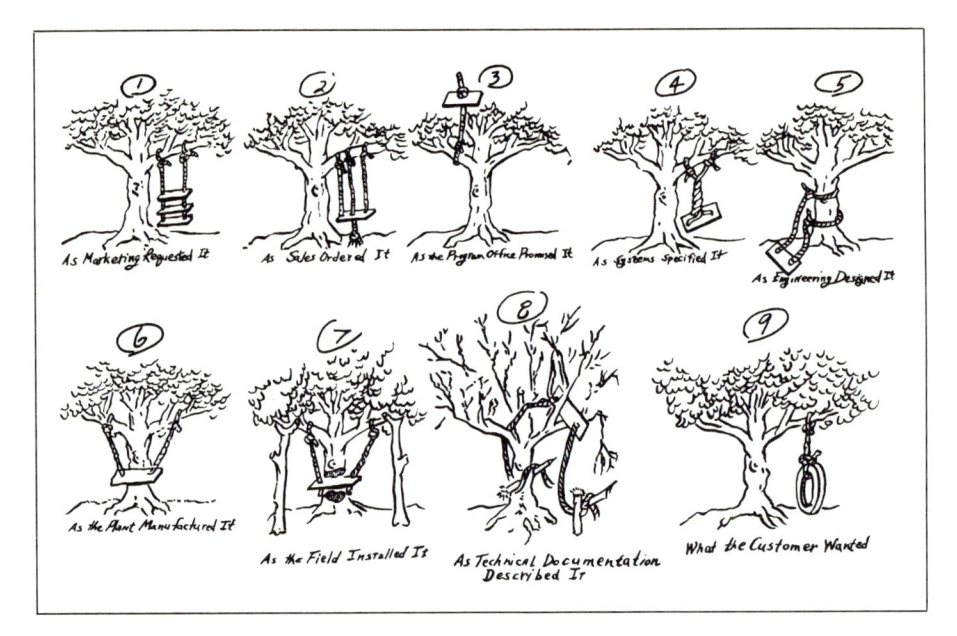

Fig. VIII-2 "Project Swing" II

Source: Allan Dundes and Carl R. Pagter, *Urban Folklore from the Paperwork Empire* (Austin, Texas, 1975). Reproduced by permission of the American Folklore Society from *Urban Folklore from the Paperwork Empire*, American Folklore Society Memoir Series, Vol. 62: 169, 1975. Not for further reproduction.

I offer in my defense, and in yours as well, evidence that the power relationships of the modern corporate world are very much on all our minds. We know them, and we care deeply about them.

Two folklorists, Allan Dundes and Carl R. Pagter, reasoning that contemporary folk culture does not move through the telling of tales and the passing on of songs, but moves by Xerox machines and office graffiti, decided to collect and to analyze such materials. Their book, *Urban Folklore from the Paperwork Empire* is a fascinating compendium of our common prejudices, anger, and humor. Consider the illustrations in Figures VIII-1 and VIII-2: perhaps you have already seen them in your office or shop.

Both cartoons tell of the frustrations of engineers, facing a bureaucratic structure. The more elaborated version (Fig. VIII-2) traces the swing through a fully developed corporate network. Reading the captions from left to right, from the top: "As marketing requested it, as sales ordered it, as the program office promised it, as systems specified it, as engineering designed it, as the plant manufactured it, as the field installed it, as technical documentation described it . . . what the customer wanted."

In Figure VIII-3, we see a folk recognition of the power position of ordinary individuals in the corporate world: Screwed.

In addition let me present a timely underground office notice which Dundes and Pagter picked up in California. Its first author, as in all folk material, is quite unknown.

NOTICE

MANY POSITIONS TO BE ELIMINATED BY MID-1967

In view of the 10% reduction of the budget, the California State Civil Service Commission will apply its RAPE program to all branches of the State Government by midsummer of 1967, according to Governor Reagan. Particular emphasis of the program will be placed on the Transportation Branch. RAPE is the designation for the phase-out of many departments and

Fig. VIII-3 "Screwed"

Source: Allan Dundes and Carl R. Pagter, *Urban Folklore from the Paperwork Empire* (Austin, Texas, 1975). Reproduced by permission of the American Folklore Society from *Urban Folklore from the Paperwork Empire*, American Folklore Society Memoir Series, Vol. 62: 153, 1975. Not for further reproduction.

stands for "Retire All Personnel Early."

Employees who are RAPED will have an opportunity to seek other employment. Those who decline to seek other employment will be able to request a review of their records before discharge. This phase of the cut-back is dubbed SCREW (Survey of Capabilities of Retired Early Workers).

One additional opportunity is promised by the Government for employees who have been RAPED or SCREWED. They may appeal for a final review . . . SHAFT. (Study by Higher Authority Following Termination.)

Governor Reagan explained that employees who are RAPED are allowed only one additional SCREWING but may request the SHAFT as many times as they desire. (p. 78)

I offer as additional evidence 40-years' experience listening to dinner-table conversations. When American working people come home for supper they don't spend a lot of time talking about fashions, sex, religion, or even politics. They often spend some time listening to or recounting their consumer adventures, enumerating the purchases and telling something of the circumstances surrounding their acquisition. But the core dinner conversation in families where only the husband works consists of a trade between husband and wife. The husband tells who said what to whom on the job, and who did what to whom, and airs his complaints, fears, and hopes. The wife responds with a similar rap about the children and her day coping with them. Now that we have more couples with both adults at work, the job tales can be exchanged from both sides of the table, and if Michael Young and Peter Willmott are right in their predictions, narratives of children's events will be ruthlessly edited.

As in the case of many subjects we have taken up previously, and especially the subjects of the family and the economy, we all know a great deal about the details of our metropolitan corporate life. We lack, however, a way of seeing our personal experience in the larger whole of the human settlement which is Boston.

In respect to our current symbolic climate our situation is much like that of our great-grandparents in Victorian times. They couldn't talk publicly about sex, although they knew a great deal about it from first-hand experience. In those days the owners of publishing firms and their editors censored books and newspapers to keep sexual topics out of the mass media. But beyond this overt censorship the authors and artists of the time lacked the necessary imagination to deal with the politics, economics, sociology, and power relationships of their contemporary sexual culture.

Our corporate taboo is the same.

Please do not mistake my argument for a simple call for more corporate news and stories. Mere multiplication of subject matter will not help us, as the endless romances of Victorian times, and the banality of socialist realism, and wartime propaganda prove. If someone knew how to summon up a successful popular art form, we would long since have drowned in propaganda.

What we require are imaginative constructs which help us to place our individual experience in the context of today's corporate metropolitan life. One critic, Robert Scholes in *Structural Fabu-*

lation, thinks that science fiction is just the form we require and that it can adequately interpret our lives to us. Whether he is right or not only time can tell. At the moment there are some books which help us. John Updike's *Couples,* from which I gave you a passage, is such a tale, although its setting is entirely suburban and domestic. Saul Bellow's *Mr. Sammler's Planet* is another such, although the portrait of New York is drawn by an old Jewish intellectual and refugee who had no corporate connections whatsoever.

I think I can make our situation still clearer to you by spending a little time analyzing the way mass fiction presents our life to us. The reason why television, movies, magazine stories, and best-sellers do not inform our world, but instead confuse it, resides in their repetition of traditional ways of looking at the world. The media do not function as windows directing our attention outwards towards meanings and relationships we have not yet seen, rather they show us what we already know.

Mass fiction functions as a mirror, constantly reflecting back to us our well-established hopes and fears. Moreover, the popular story is a special kind of mirror, a mirror for strangers, because it focuses upon individuals and their separateness. Thereby it reinforces our isolation one from another.

Realism, the use of costumes, language, and scenes which replicate details from the contemporary world, is the dominant convention of our film and printed fiction. We are used to such a presentation and are comfortable in launching our fantasies from such a platform. But it is not the verisimilitude which captures our attention. Rather the fantasies themselves, the plots, the action, the tales, constitute our pleasure. And if the story is to expand our awareness, it does so not by the paraphernalia of its realism, but by the logic of its action. Who does what, and how it all takes place, are the things that teach us something.

Family situations, love stories, and male adventure tales currently dominate television. There is nothing new in this programming; the same trio comprised most of our fantasy during the twenties when commonplace fiction poured from the movies, magazines, and cheap books. The happy ending is also a stock convention, like realism, as much employed then as now.

The sameness which pervades the entire fifty years of our study comes from the plots written within the three broad action settings. The plots recapitulate our national dreams and nightmares, they mirror our personal hopes and fears. The protagonists in all these stories are the dreams and the nightmares, not the actuality of human situations. The hero or heroine struggles against failure in the race for social mobility, against the revelation of cowardice, against social rejection, against male and female dependency, against the female inability to find a safe protector. The heroes and heroines do not struggle towards love, mastery, and understanding of the world. They labor in the bog of power and powerlessness.

The individualization of the plots, the lone American confronting his dreams and nightmares, represents a core tradition in our culture. This focus holds our attention because we know the feelings so well. But this individualization is also the isolating force of popular fiction, whether that fiction comes towards us from the television set, a movie screen, a magazine, or a book. By ceaseless repetition of this basic formula the media screen from us alternative visions of the world and alternative fantasies and nightmares. I suspect also by constantly stressing the necessity for individual struggles in a world we all know to be made up of large forces and giant institutions, the formula heightens our personal guilt and anxiety, and thereby further estranges us from our world.

Let us examine a successful soap opera to see just how popular fiction works. The author, Olive Higgins Prouty (1882-1974), spent her entire life within the Boston BEA, except for four years at Smith College. She was no cynical professional grinding out material she did not believe in. She wrote many popular books and in all she attempted, she says in her memoir, *Pencil Shavings,* to tell a story about families which portrayed what she thought were significant aspects of life in her day. Ms. Prouty's motives were not unusual. The sheer volume of media products is too large for it to be the work of a coterie of professionals. Most of it comes from the pens of writers who are describing the world as they see it, and most of this output is screened by editors who examine their own personal judgment about what is truth, as well as about what will sell.

In choosing a soap opera, I do not mean to single out women's fiction for ridicule. We could as well have carried out the same analysis of popular nightmares with George V. Higgins, *The Friends of Eddie Coyle* (1970). But I find the soaps more interesting than shoot-em-up male adventure stories. The soaps, after all, include men as well as women, while the cowboy and crime stories generally restrict themselves to male characters, horses, and machines.

The soap, *Stella Dallas*, first appeared as a serial novel in a mass-circulation, middle-class monthly, the *American Magazine*, the first installment in October 1922. Houghton Mifflin brought it out as a book in 1923. In January 1924 the story was rewritten and produced as a play, but it did not succeed in this form, according to Ms. Prouty, because the leading actress misinterpreted the character of Stella. In 1925 Samuel Goldwyn made a silent picture of the tale with Ronald Coleman playing Stella's husband and Douglas Fairbanks, Jr., in the role of Stella's daughter's suitor. In 1937 Goldwyn remade it as a talking picture with Barbara Stanwyck cast as Stella. Perhaps the novel's best remembered form was as a radio serial. In 1935 the Phillips Milk of Magnesia company bought the rights for *Stella Dallas* from a fraudulent promoter, and professional radio writers wrote endless dialogue for a daily soap opera which played to enormous radio audiences from 1935 until 1953. The axis of dramatic tension in the radio series turned around the conflicts between a working-class mother, Stella, and her socialite daughter, Laurel.

Stella Dallas evokes the dreams and nightmares of social mobility. The setting is a New England mill town, like Worcester, Massachusetts, where Ms. Prouty was raised and where her family triumphed in business. Stella is the daughter of a millworker, a pretty, goodhearted, cheerful, and ambitious girl. Upon her return home from Normal School she sets her net to catch a husband.

> Stella was born in one of those ugly three-deckers, close to the mill gate. She was ten years old when her father bought one of the red cottage-houses on the river-bank. She had been proud of the cottage then, and proud of it too, as she grew older. On each side of the little porch over the front door, every spring, for years, Stella planted morning-glories and wild-cucumber vine, which climbed a strong trellis of her own making. . . .
>
> She had trained the docile vines to run all over the picket fence that surrounded the little house, and had shrouded the back porch with them; had shrouded with them, too, a latticed summer-house which stood in the side yard. Stella had copied the summer-house, with much the same genius with which she copied hats or dresses, from a summer-house she had seen in Millhampton across the river.
>
> The first night Stephen called on Stella, he had sat in the hammock alone, while Stella had curled herself up on the low step of the summer-house, leaning her head against one of the upright posts, so that the searchlight moon could shine full upon her face, and her caller could observe from the darkness of the hammock how pretty she was. (pp. 77-78)

Her husband-to-be, Stephen Dallas, is a midwestern knight, temporarily in disguise. Stephen, fleeing the family seat in Illinois because of his father's fraud and suicide, appears in Cataract Village, Millhampton, by the accident of a help-wanted advertisement. A lonely bookkeeper in the local mills, he is an easy target for Stella.

Stella and Stephen meet at a Congregational Church supper. She is the prettiest and cleverest girl in the village, he the most eligible bachelor. They marry and prosper together, for a time. Stephen recovers from the weight of guilt, studies the law at night, and becomes counsel for the firm. They have a daughter, Laurel, in whom Stella, after Stephen leaves her, invests her entire life.

Why the separation? A fatal flaw prevents Stella's parallel social progress. She cannot overcome the habits of a lifetime in the working class. She is too forward, too brassy, and too flirtatious to be accepted by "Worcester" Society. She persists in behaving inappropriately and her way of life drives Stephen away. He is, after all, a refined and sensitive young man. He is not climbing a social ladder, but assuming his rightful place. Like Nick Carraway in *The Great Gatsby* he is one of America's small class of true gentlemen, the son of old professional money. His business career serves only to test his manhood, and his success proves his inherent virtue.

At the opening of the novel Stella is travelling with Laurel from one fashionable seaside hotel to another. She is presenting her daughter to the wealthy as best she can. Laurel, now eleven years old, also goes for three weeks each summer to stay with her father in New York where he has now established a successful law practice. Stephen is wealthy once more, and has resumed a courtship of his childhood sweetheart from Illinois, a Mrs. Morrison, herself now become a rich widow. Mrs. Morrison is gently bred, beautiful, and gracious, and lives in tasteful luxury on Long Island. She has three sons, but her daughter died in infancy. Stella's only power in this situation consists of her threatening the scandal of a publicly contested divorce.

Most of the lines of the book lovingly describe property, and celebrate the Eden of tasteful, as opposed to nouveau, or middle-class wealth.

Laurel pays her first visit to widow Morrison's Long Island home.

> There was a tea-table, with a white cloth near one of the windows, with shining silver on it, and shining tea-cups and a plate or two of snowy sandwiches and a basket of frosted cakes. . . .
>
> Upstairs, inside the most exquisite little bathroom Laurel had ever stepped foot in—creamy tiles clear to the ceiling, creamy floor, creamy fittings, not a scrap of nickel in sight—everything all smooth shining porcelain, like the inside of a beautiful china cup. . . .
>
> Very carefully Laurel followed her directions, gazing wonderingly about her as she did so, examining various details with investigating nose and fingertips; sniffing the soap; ever so cautiously opening the door of the medicine chest; touching with gentle forefinger the silk window-hangings in the bedroom; touching with the same gentle forefinger its ivory colored walls; the shade on the lamp, on the table between the the two beds. It was made of real filet! So too were the curious little pillows on the beds. . . . So too, was the bureau-scarf, and the tidy on the back of the big winged-chair by the window. All real filet! And just the simplest piece of filet cost sixty-five cents in the neckwear department! . . .
>
> It was like a scene at the 'movies,' with all those books, and the piano, and the comfortable chairs, and the big portrait hanging over the fireplace, and the pretty lady behind the steaming tea-kettle, and the dog, and the boys. . . . She, standing on the outside, was the only unreal thing in this home scene." (pp. 40-42)

Such descriptions are held together by the dramatic tension of Stella's passion for the social advancement of her daughter. In the end Stella makes a bargain with Mrs. Morrison. She will grant a divorce, if Mrs. Morrison will agree to raise Laurel and to introduce her into New York Society. Such a mother's sacrifice, however, does not suffice. Laurel, out of loyalty, refuses to leave, although she is fascinated by Mrs. Morrison, and instead threatens to take a job as a secretary in a downtown Boston office and to continue living with her mother. Panicked by this threat to her dream, Stella drives her daughter away by marrying a former stablemaster she had been flirting with, a man Laurel detests, indeed he has by now become a drunk.

The book ends with Mrs. Morrison's marriage to Stephen Dallas, and her staging of a debutante party for Laurel. The servants have been instructed to leave the shades up on the side of the New York mansion which faces an alley. Stella returns from a long day's work in the shirt-waist factory where she must now labor to support her husband. She stops off at her one-room tenement flat to find him asleep in an alchoholic stupor, and then goes on uptown to stand in the alley, looking in on her daughter's triumph.

> Stella had never seen her more beautiful. Her dress was white, chiffon, she thought, made over something silvery, that made her shine as if there was dew all over her. No dress Stella had ever provided for Laurel could *touch* this. One of those artists, whose address only the few fortunate possess, had made this fairy gown for Laurel, Stella guessed. My, how she became it! Gosh! She looked like a regular queen to-night!
>
> She carried a sheaf of white orchids on her left arm. Through the chiffon ribbon that tied the flowers Stella caught a glimpse of something that looked like diamonds sparkling on Laurel's wrist! A moment later, as Laurel turned a little, she caught a glimpse of what was clasped about her throat. Pearls! A string of pearls! . . .
>
> For more than an hour Stella stood in the shadow of an electric pole, and feasted and feasted. A policeman finally discovered her and told her to move along.
>
> "All right," she replied cheerfully, "I will. I'm ready now. I've seen enough." (pp. 301-303)

I think we would be well repaid with insight into how our culture works if we spent some time figuring out why such a plot and such descriptive detail no longer move us. Today Ms. Prouty's fantasies are not credible, yet we still consume billions of words and pictures devoted to the same theme: the nightmares of social mobility.

It is an easier task to guess why the book enjoyed such popularity in its day. What working-class family has not lost a child whose desired success carried the child beyond sympathy for its parents? *Stella Dallas* is thus an immigrant story, and a native American story as well. And who among us does not carry some childhood class flaw which, despite our best efforts, betrays us in situations we care most about? And who among us does not feel that at the center of his or her being lies a core of virtue and love which, far from being recognized and rewarded by others, forces us to sacrifice and to suffer the injustices of everyday life?

These questions, it seems to me, explain the bond between Ms. Prouty and her readers. But more directly relevant to our understanding of the metropolitan symbolic climate in which we live, is the matter of the dream of mobility itself. Where is Stella's sacrifice, Mrs. Morrison's generosity, and Laurel's youthful beauty taking this young girl? As the novel ends Laurel is speeding down a track to marriage to a son of an old and wealthy New York family. She will realize a dream of power and narcissism. Daisy Buchanan meet Laurel Grosvenor! She will be a winner in a 200,000,000-person race.

It is a mindless dream of property and power. It is the very tradition which Fitzgerald said corrupted American society, and which Mumford saw as threatening to destroy human life itself.

No survey of the functioning of the media as a mirror for our dreams and nightmares could be complete without at least a brief review of the advertisements which accompany our fiction. Every hour's television and radio, and most every page of our magazines and newspapers carry the fantasies of the advertisers alongside the fantasies of the broadcasters and publishers. Not surprisingly, since both groups are seeking a favorable response from mass audiences, the storylines are much the same. The only disjunction I discovered occurred during Prohibition when the stories were full of alcohol but only soft drinks could be advertised.

I have not been able to carry this research very far, but I have made some comparisons among the most successful magazines of the twenties and some of the most popular recent ones. The beginning findings are that the symbolic climate in which we live has not substantially changed over the past 50 years. We dwell in the same fantasy smog our parents did.

This constancy has been sustained despite drastic shifts in the media which carry the fantasies. During the 1920's mass, middle-class-oriented magazines printed an enormous volume of fiction. General magazines carried men's and women's stories in the same periodical. I have selected examples from the monthly, *American Magazine* for 1922, and from the weekly, *Collier's,* for 1926.

The continued advance of movies and the introduction of radio crowded magazines out of fiction, and more and more they turned to nonfiction. The years from 1930-1950 marked the apogee of picture and news magazines like *Life* and *Time*. Television further accelerated this trend towards nonfiction, and also encouraged specialization among magazines. Television took the general audience, magazines sought special interest groups. *Life, Look*, and the *Saturday Evening Post, Collier's* and the *American*, all have folded.

Today's fiction, thus, appears in magazines designed for very particular audiences. I have selected *McCall's* in 1960 as a woman's journal, indeed it was the magazine which coined a promotional slogan, "togetherness," in the 1950's, a phrase we now use to characterize that incontinent decade. I have also looked at *True* for 1972. It is a men's adventure magazine which turns factual tales into fiction formats. To find a continuation of the men's fiction tradition I have also been reading *Playboy* for 1974. *Playboy* presents more fiction and sells it to a larger audience than all the other men's magazines together.

By restricting this review to magazines I have unavoidably introduced a distortion into our history. A straight track of popular tales would travel from the general magazines of the twenties to the radio scripts of the thirties, forties, and fifties, and then to television. The mechanics of obtaining scripts, however, forbade my undertaking such a task. Perhaps as you look at the images I am going to show you, you could hold them up in your mind against what you now see on television and thereby test for any possible distortions which come from the magazine format.

Since both editors and advertisers seek to reach the largest possible audience both must employ common tactics. Both choose fiction, either in the mode of conventional stories, or in the form of story pictures which offer varying amounts of text. The choice of fiction is not accidental, but at the heart of the drive for the largest possible audience.

By definition fiction is make-believe. It does not purport to tell the reader or beholder what actually happens, or happened. Through this convention the audience is freed momentarily to suspend its judgment about what it knows in fact happens in the world it inhabits. By this device author and reader are allowed a meeting in fantasy. The advantage the convention offers to authors with commercial goals and with large audiences in mind lies in the consequence that make-believe may often be much more universal than the facts of class-, race-, and sex-bound experience. Neither the poor man, nor the rich may be put off by luxury, women can participate in adventure and violence, blacks in white romance. After all, none of it is true.

Having made the choice for fiction, editors and advertisers then proceed to find fantasies which they think will be as close to universal as they can guess. Hence the fantasies of magazines dwell on the inescapable biologic cycles of humans—courtship, marriage, children, death. Since the first three groups of fantasies also represent ages of heavy purchasing, fantasy and commerce converge. Because ours are American magazines, the biologic fantasies are also intertwined with other common cultural themes—especially individual striving for class advancement. In all of this both aspirations and fears, dreams and nightmares, are touched upon. Necessarily, because they live together, many of the men's and the women's fantasies are complementary. They describe roles that fit together to make an American family. Perhaps most surprising, given the extraordinary

Fig. VIII-4

Source: *Playboy* (October 1974). Copyright © 1974 by Playboy.

changes in the real world, is the constancy of the fantasies presented by the magazines from 1920 to the present.

Young men, of course, have sexual fantasies of attracting many beautiful women, but an American young man is in addition a man who lusts after property. Here (Fig. VIII-4) we meet the nineteenth-century preoccupation with things in a contemporary form.

Alternatively the American male has been the solitary hero, pitting himself against a hostile nature in the wilderness (Fig. VIII-5). Such a man is, perhaps, not yet ready for marriage.

Fig. VIII-5
Source: *True* (March 1972). Courtesy of True Magazine.

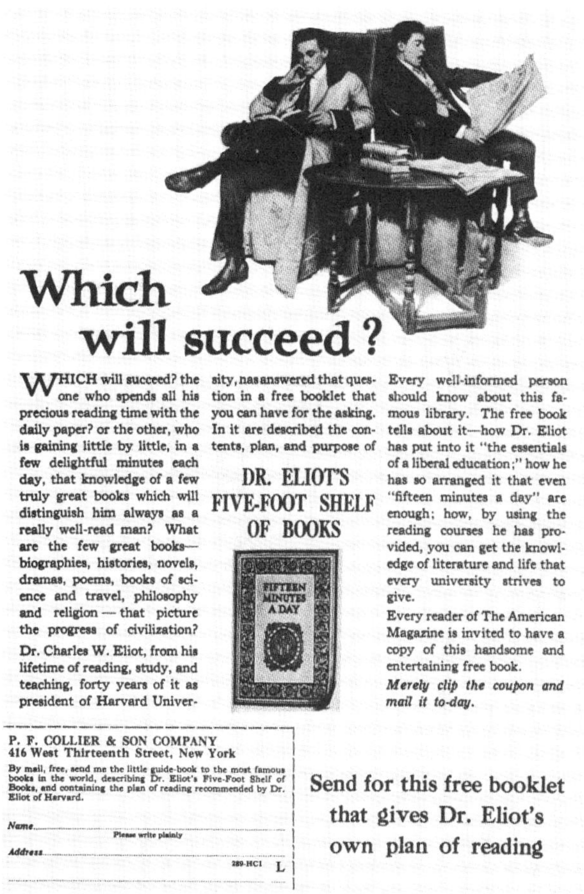

Fig. VIII-6
Source: *American Magazine* (July 1922). Courtesy of Macmillan, Inc.

During the nineteenth century as more and more American boys found themselves confined to factory benches, store counters, and office desks, the fantasy of the wilderness rose in popularity. However, a more realistic fantasy suggested successful competition for those few jobs which offered good pay and more personal freedom. Educators advertised that they had a fool-proof method for beating out the competition (Figs. VIII-6 and VIII-7).

94 THE WAY WE LIVE

Fig. VIII-7

Source: *True* (March 1972). Courtesy of International Correspondence Schools, Inc.

Fig. VIII-8

Source: *Collier's Magazine* (July 3, 1926). Courtesy of The Gillette Company.

Fig. VIII-9

Source: *Playboy* (November 1974). Courtesy of 21 Brands, Inc.

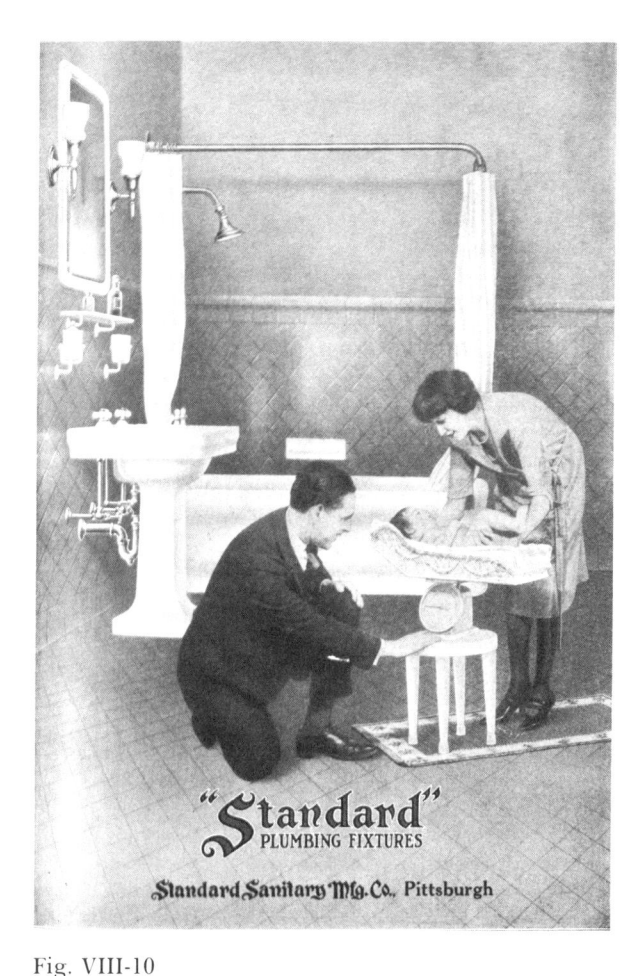

Fig. VIII-10

Source: *American Magazine* (August 1922). Courtesy of American Standard, Inc.

The universal appeal of self-education as a route to advancement, however, suffered from the social knowledge that college boys started the race ahead of the others. For noncollege readers, then, appeals to the class standing of the Ivy League colleges thus simultaneously embodied dreams and nightmares. Yet because of their use of widely recognized stereotypes of upper-class life, the college advertisement tantalizes now as it did in the less-educated years of the twenties (Figs. VIII-8 and VIII-9).

After youth came marriage and the young man assumed the role of provider. Surely he will want his wife to have advantages in the house his mother didn't (Fig. VIII-10).

96 THE WAY WE LIVE

Fig. VIII-11
Source: *Playboy* (November 1974). Courtesy of VISA, U.S.A., Inc.

Fig. VIII-12
Source: *Collier's Magazine* (July 10, 1926). Courtesy of Chevrolet Division of General Motors Corporation.

Fig. VIII-13
Source: *True* (March 1972). Courtesy of Chevrolet Division of General Motors Corporation.

And surely he will want to express his love for his child in ways they both understand—things (Fig. VIII-11).

Wife and child, of course, will find happiness when he purchases and drives an automobile. Note here (Fig. VIII-12) that the husband is an isolated figure, waving to them, while mother and children prepare for the oncoming family picnic.

The proliferation of the automobile has distorted family automobile advertising in our time. A car is now assumed to be as much a fixture in the American family as a toilet. Hence the same appeal, the picnic, the outdoors, is now presented to youthful couples, presumably not married, certainly without children (Fig. VIII-13). The attempt is to drive this expensive appliance down into the courtship age. Conceivably a father could have bought the machine for his son's entertainment.

Fig. VIII-14

Source: *American Magazine* (July 1922).

Fig. VIII-15

Source: *American Magazine* (August 1922). Courtesy of the Liggett Group, Inc. All rights reserved. Copyright by Liggett Group, Inc.

During the twenties successful businessmen served as important fantasy figures. Here (Fig. VIII-14) a dour gentleman of a lifetime of unremitting work, the inventor of the automatic bottle-blowing machine, is offered as an example for imitation. True fact and opinion are adapted to a life-story format.

The same fantasy model is softened, made more youthful and etherealized by Fatima Cigarettes (Fig. VIII-15).

A contemporary 1920's cartoon (Fig. VIII-16) doubts that the fantasy of business success adequately represents the trends of society.

Fig. VIII-16

Source: *Collier's Magazine* (July 10, 1926).

98 THE WAY WE LIVE

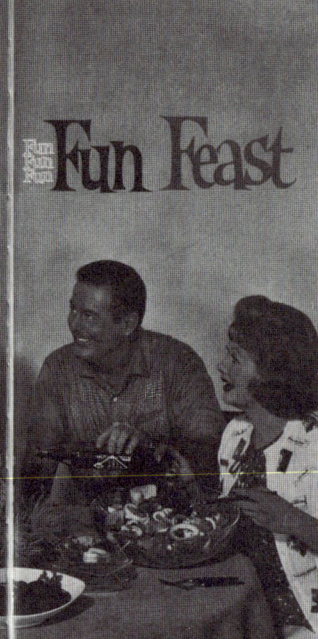

Fig. VIII-17

Source: *McCall's* (October 1960). Courtesy of McCall's Magazine. Copyright 1960 by the McCall Publishing Company.

Fig. VIII-18

Source: *Playboy* (November 1974). Courtesy of Hyatt Corporation.

Since the Great Depression businessmen no longer serve as fantasy objects and instead advertisers have substituted the creatures of the media themselves, entertainers and sports figures (Fig. VIII-17). Their message is often reversed so the hero does not suggest we might be like him, but rather that he is like us.

In fact a cynicism has pervaded our cult of individual achievement and class success so that the fantasy is most often presented in a blurred fa-

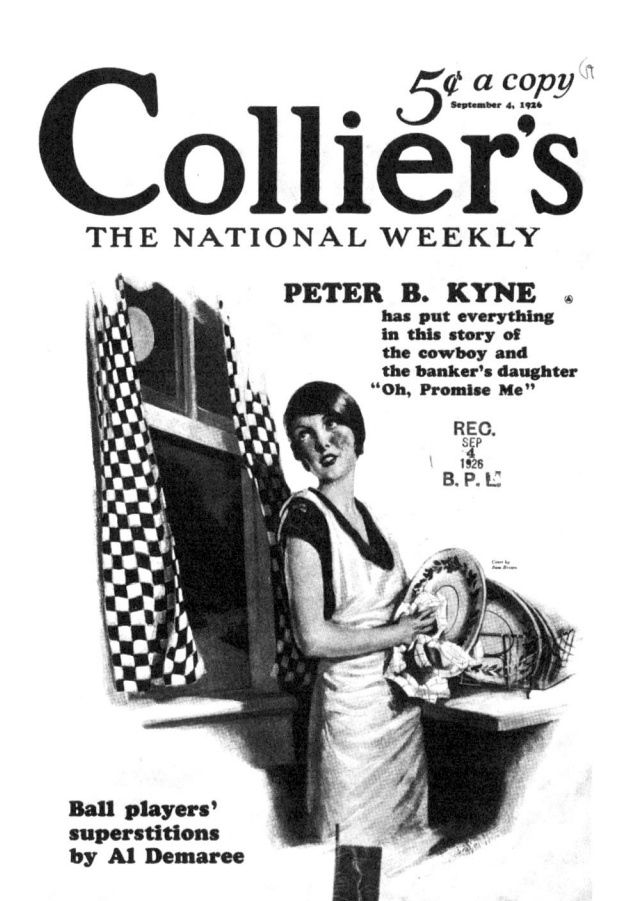

Fig. VIII-19

Source: *Collier's* Magazine (September 4, 1926).

Teeth You Envy
Are brushed in this new way

Millions of people daily now combat the film on teeth. This method is fast spreading all the world over, largely by dental advice.

You see the results in every circle. Teeth once dingy now glisten as they should. Teeth once concealed now show in smiles.

This is to offer a ten-day test to prove the benefits to you.

That cloudy film

A dingy film accumulates on teeth. When fresh it is viscous—you can feel it. Film clings to teeth, gets between the teeth and stays. It forms the basis of cloudy coats.

Film is what discolors—not the teeth. Tartar is based on film. Film holds food substance which ferments and forms acid. It holds the acid in contact with the teeth to cause decay.

Millions of germs breed in it. They, with tartar, are the chief cause of pyorrhea. Thus most tooth troubles are now traced to film, and very few escape them.

Must be combated

Film has formed a great tooth problem. No ordinary tooth paste can effectively combat it. So dental science has for years sought ways to fight this film.

Two ways have now been found. Able authorities have proved them by many careful tests. A new tooth paste has been perfected, to comply with modern requirements. And these two film combatants are embodied in it.

This tooth paste is Pepsodent, now employed by forty races, largely by dental advice.

Other tooth enemies

Starch is another tooth enemy. It gums the teeth, gets between the teeth, and often ferments and forms acid.

Nature puts a starch digestant in the saliva to digest those starch deposits, but with modern diet it is often too weak.

Pepsodent multiplies that starch digestant with every application. It also multiplies the alkalinity of the saliva. That is Nature's neutralizer for acids which cause decay.

Thus Pepsodent brings effects which modern authorities desire. They are bringing to millions a new dental era. Now we ask you to watch those effects for a few days and learn what they mean to you.

The facts are most important to you. Cut out the coupon now.

10-Day Tube Free

THE PEPSODENT COMPANY,
Dept. 62, 1104 S. Wabash Ave., Chicago, Ill.
Mail 10-day tube of Pepsodent to

Only one tube to a family.

Pepsodent
The New-Day Dentifrice

Endorsed by modern authorities and now advised by leading dentists nearly all the world over. All druggists supply the large tubes.

Fig. VIII-20

Source: *American Magazine* (July 1922). Courtesy Lever Brothers Co.

---

shion. Today's message is more indirect and magical than the old one. It says one need not struggle to be a success, one can instead buy a little of the sensation (Fig. VIII-18).

Women's dreams are presented as complementary to the men's. A young woman, home washing dishes, dreams of love (Fig. VIII-19).

She does, of course, suffer the nightmare of sexual competition (Fig. VIII-20).

Fig. VIII-21

Source: *Collier's Magazine* (July 24, 1926).

Fig. VIII-22

Source: *McCall's* (October 1960). Courtesy of McCall's Magazine. Copyright 1960 by the McCall Publishing Company.

Fig. VIII-23

Source: *McCall's* (October 1960). Courtesy McCall's Magazine. Copyright 1960 by the McCall Publishing Company.

Fig. VIII-24

Source: *McCall's* (October 1960). Courtesy of General Foods, Inc.

Yet all American women are supposed to feel that they harbor within them an inner virtue which despite all vicissitudes will ultimately be recognized in a successful marriage. This fantasy is the counterpart of the male fantasy of the hard-working boy being recognized by the boss, rising to financial success, and marrying a woman of higher class. Here (Fig. VIII-21) Kathleen Norris offers a tale of many tribulations and final triumph.

A smart, fashionable, college-educated, New York working girl struggles with her feelings of turmoil and inadequacy towards a successful conclusion of marriage to an up-and-coming aristocratic young New York lawyer (Fig. VIII-22).

Once married the woman helps the man to realize his economic potential. Here (Fig. VIII-23) the Stella Dallas plot is reworked for a happy ending. The rich boy is bankrupted by his parents' spendthrift ways. His wife and the former family butler help him to find wealth and power once again. The story opens with a listing of the price of the ranch house and an enumeration of its furnishings.

General Foods advertises (Fig. VIII-24) for the same family life.

Fig. VIII-25

Source: *Collier's Magazine* (September 25, 1926).

Fig. VIII-26

Source: *McCall's* (October 1960). Courtesy of McCall's Magazine. Copyright 1960 by the McCall Publishing Company.

Although the married woman's fantasy role remains unchanged over the fifty years, the setting for the fantasies enjoys heavy capital investments. First the white steel enamel cabinets (Fig. VIII-25), then the elaborated fusion of dining room and kitchen (Fig. VIII-26).

The opposite of the blurring of the success drive for men is the massive and sustained use of narcissistic fantasies for women. Here (Fig. VIII-27) is a modest one, looking stylish in Paris in a new dress one made oneself.

One of the surprises of this brief research was the discovery of a series of stories and advertisements which recorded the blending of masculine fears with American traditions. Here is the record of one of the American nightmares.

An early twentieth-century hero, President Theodore Roosevelt, was the subject of countless newspaper and magazine features. The cult of Teddy was like the cult of Jack Kennedy today. Roosevelt wrapped himself in the mantle of the West and in a two-part feature by his butler it is revealed that the pistol in the picture (Fig. VIII-28) was kept by the President under his pillow all the time he lived in the White House. To ward off what, one wonders.

A contemporary advertisement (Fig. VIII-29) parallels this situation with a picture of the laying of the railroads in the West. The builders are armed although the Indians in the distance look peaceful enough. Purchase of a pistol is urged as a necessary tool of civilized life.

But the city is now where most of the magazine's readers live. In a feature story on the invention and proliferation of the military machine gun the author suggests the nightmare of urban wars between gangsters and police (Fig. VIII-30).

Fig. VIII-27
Source: *McCall's* (October 1960). Courtesy of McCall's Magazine. Copyright 1960 by the McCall Publishing Company.

Fig. VIII-29
Source: *Collier's Magazine* (July 10, 1926). Courtesy Colt Industries, Inc.

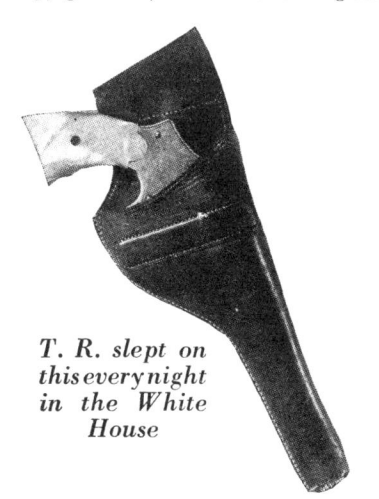

Fig. VIII-28
Source: *Collier's Magazine* (August 7, 1926).

Fig. VIII-30
Source: *Collier's Magazine* (December 4, 1926).

104　THE WAY WE LIVE

Brink's Fleet Carries thirty million dollars a day

Fig. VIII-31

Source: *Collier's Magazine* (September 4, 1926). Courtesy of International Harvester, Inc.

How Jones felt the first time he took his wife's dog out for a walk

Fig. VIII-32

Source: *Collier's Magazine* (July 10, 1926).

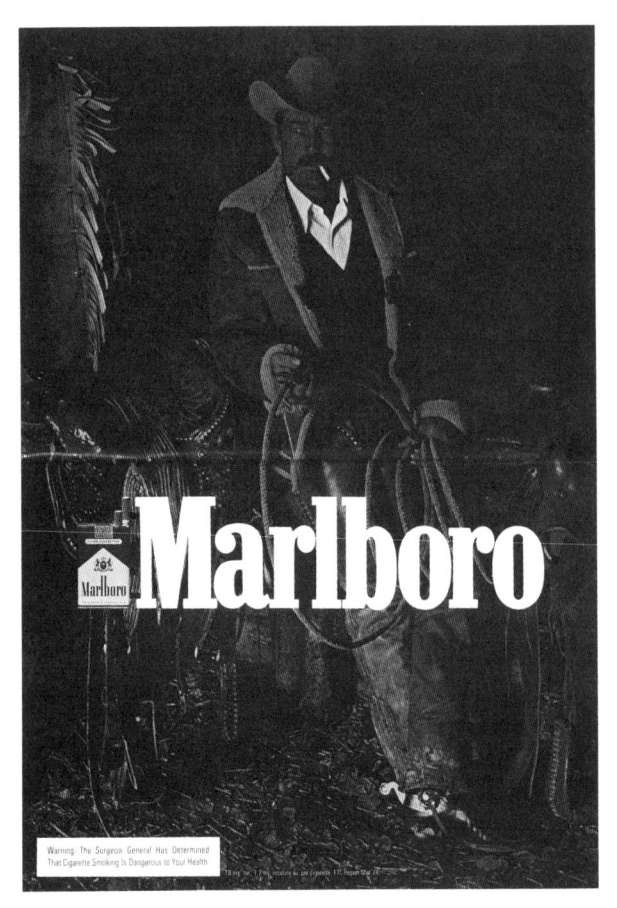

Fig. VIII-33

Source: *Playboy* (October 1974). Courtesy of Philip Morris, Inc.

International Harvester in an advertisement for trucks pictures an urban class war (Fig. VIII-31): the giant mills, the workers lining up to get their pay at an armored truck guarded by men with guns drawn.

The reality of the danger from Indians, machine guns, and class wars in the modern American city seems at best slight, and one guesses that readers knew that. These fantasies were perhaps attended to for other reasons (Fig. VIII-32).

The revival of the lonely western hero, the Marlboro Man (Fig. VIII-33), in our own time suggests that sex, not physical danger is what is at issue in these nightmare stories and advertisements.

Fig. VIII-34

Source: *True* (March 1972).
Courtesy of U.S. Army Recruiting Command.

Think enormous.

Small cars are making it. The M60-A1 is 27 feet long, 12 feet wide and weighs 52.5 tons, loaded.

Flashy colors are in. The M60-A1 gives you a choice of one. An odd, brownish green.

Gas economy is a must. At 3 gallons to the mile, it's not one of our best selling features.

But talk about power. The M60-A1 offers a 750-horse, 12-cylinder air-cooled engine and cross-drive transmission as standard equipment.

And maneuverability. The M60-A1 turns on a dime. Large, but a dime.

And ease of parking. Who's going to fight you for a spot?

The M60-A1. It isn't small. It isn't flashy. It isn't even economical.

It's just enormous.

If you have the bug to move to something bigger, see your nearest Army representative. He'll tell you about the opportunities to make it big. In Armor.

Today's Army wants to join you.

Fig. VIII-35

Source: *Playboy* (November 1974).
Courtesy of Harley Davidson, Inc.

An Army recruiting advertisement (Fig. VIII-34) published during the Vietnam War, but not mentioning it, lends support to our interpretation.

All fantasies are in danger of collapsing by the attenuation of their own logic, or by their failure to energize their readers' own fantasy life. I find the gun and western hero sexual nightmare dissolving into comedy in this motorcycle advertisement (Fig. VIII-35). Our hero, dressed in emblematic costume, drinks his beer in prideful embarrassment while his friends come to admire his new bike. But the dancing figures of the boys and girls coming from the background suggest to me that they are where life and happiness lie, and that our hero will soon be left solitary with his beer and his big machine.

In conclusion, let me say that I don't find in any of this material which comes towards us in such unremitting flow, either information or imagination which helps me understand the metropolitan world in which I live. Instead I experience a relentless prodding towards the narrow confines of personal power and narcissism. The slight changes in style and the increase in vagueness and etherealization represent no gain either to my cognition or imagination of life. Rather I find myself being pushed aside by the media so that I must see and experience my world as an isolated individual. I know this condition is neither a social fact nor a representation of the richness of life here in Boston.

Our problem today is to understand how we really live. It is not an easy task, in part because our communications system is geared to obscuring and confusing our view. It is also not an easy task because our world is organized on such a large scale. I find it hard to think and to speak about a city of six million Bostonians, even in the sketchy way our four topics have allowed. You may have found my reasoning often hard to follow, and often incorrect. It must necessarily be so until many of us can imagine more boldly, and define more clearly, how our lives are connected one to another. I have the faith that as we penetrate the smog of our traditional fantasies and commercial messages, the clarity will help to make ours a much more humane city in which to live.

For the moment, let me close with a metaphor which stands for what I think we will discover to be the relationship between our lives and the Boston metropolis. The passage is taken from a science fiction love story "Slow Sculpture," published by Theodore Sturgeon in 1971.

He came out into the entrance court and contemplated his bonsai.

Early sun gold-frosted the horizontal upper foliage of the old tree and brought its gnarled limbs into sharp relief, tough brown-gray and crevices of velvet. Only the companion of a bonsai (there are owners of bonsai, but they are a lesser breed) fully understands the relationship. There is an exclusive and individual treeness to the tree because it is a living thing, and living things change, and there are definite ways in which the tree desires to change. A man sees the tree, and in his mind makes certain extensions and extrapolations of what he sees, and sets about making them happen. The tree in turn will do only what a tree can do, will resist to the death any attempt to do what it cannot do, or do in less time than it needs. The shaping of a bonsai is therefore always a compromise and always a cooperation. A man cannot create a bonsai, nor can a tree; it takes both, and they must understand each other. It takes a long time to do that. One memorizes one's bonsai, every twig, the angle of every crevice and needle, and, lying awake at night or in a pause a thousand miles away, one recalls this or that line or mass, one makes one's plans. With wire and water and light, with tilting and with the planting of water-robbing weeds or heavy root-shading ground cover, one explains to the tree what one wants, and if the explanation is well enough made, and there is great enough understanding, the tree will respond and obey—almost. Always there will be its own self-respecting, highly individual variation: *Very well, I shall do what you want, but I will do it in* my *way.* And for these variations, the tree is always willing to present a clear and logical explanation, and more often than not (almost smiling) it will make clear to the man that he could have avoided it if his understanding had been better.

It is the slowest sculpture in the world, and there is, at times, doubt as to which is being sculpted, man or tree. (pp. 88-89)

Reference Bibliography

(Citations appear in the order in which they are mentioned in the text.)

CHAPTER II.

Raymond Williams, *Keywords: A Vocabulary of Culture and Society* (New York, 1976).

Michael Young and Peter Willmott, *The Symmetrical Family* (New York, 1973).

Joseph F. Kett, *Rites of Passage: Adolescence in America, 1790 to the Present* (New York, 1977), Chapter 1.

Michael Young and Peter Willmott, *Family and Kinship in East London* (Baltimore, 1957).

United States Bureau of the Census, *Current Population Reports*, Series P-20, No. 287, "Marital Status and Living Arrangements, March 1975" (Washington, 1975), p. 5

CHAPTER III.

United States Department of Commerce, Bureau of Economic Analysis, *One-Percent Sample, Continuous Work History, Boston BEA, Non-Migrants, 1970.*

United States Bureau of the Census, *Statistical Abstract: 1971* (Washington, 1972), Table 577, p. 374.

Lester C. Thurow, *Generating Inequality: Mechanisms of Distribution in the United States Economy* (New York, 1975).

CHAPTER IV.

Robert W. Eisenmenger, *The Dynamics of Growth in the New England Economy* (Middletown, Conn., 1967).

United States Department of Commerce, Bureau of Economic Analysis, *One-Percent Sample, Continuous Work History, Boston BEA, Longitudinal Analysis, 1960-1970.*

United States Bureau of the Census, *Census of Population: 1930* (Washington, 1933), Vol. 3, Table 10.

———, *Census of the Population: 1970*, Vol. 1, *Characteristics of the Population* (Washington, 1973), Parts 23, 31, 41, Table 183.

Charles E. Artman, "New England's Industrial Prospects," in American Geographical Society, *New England's Prospect: 1933*, Special Publication No. 16 (New York, 1933), pp. 50-64.

Harold Latham, "Massachusetts Still a Leader," *Industrial Development and Manufacturers Record*, 133 (September, 1964), p. 36.

Bennett Harrison, *The Economic Development of Massachusetts*, Report to the Joint Committee on Commerce and Labor, Massachusetts State Legislature (Boston, November 1974).

Pearson Product Moment Correlations from United States Department of Commerce, Bureau of Economic Analysis, *Ten-Percent Sample, Continuous Work History, Boston BEA Counties, 1969.*

CHAPTER V.

Sam Bass Warner, Jr., *Streetcar Suburbs: The Process of Growth in Boston, 1870-1900* (Cambridge, 1962).

Henry David Thoreau, *The Journal*, Bradford Torrey and Francis H. Allen, eds. (Boston, 1906), entry for May 9, 1852, vol. IV, pp. 41-42.

Laura Wood Roper, *FLO: A Biography of Frederick Law Olmsted* (Baltimore, 1973).

Albert Fein, *Frederick Law Olmsted and the American Environmental Tradition* (New York, 1972).

Reid A. Bryson and John E. Kutzbach, *Air Pollution*, Association of American Geographers, Committee on College Geography, Resource Paper No. 2 (Washington, 1968).

Thomas R. Detwyler and Melvin G. Marcus, *Urbanization and the Environment* (Scituate, Mass., 1972).

Nancy M. Page and Richard W. Weaver, Jr., *Wild Plants in the City* (New York, 1975).

John Rublowsky, *Nature in the City* (New York, 1967), p. 122.

Charles Dickens, *American Notes for General Circulation* (1842, reprint Gloucester, Mass., 1968), p. 41.

Boston 200, Neighborhood History Series, *East Boston* (Boston, 1976), p. 12, Lexington St.

Thomas S. Elias and Howard C. Irwin, "Urban Trees," *Scientific American*, 235 (November, 1976), pp. 110-118.

Don Gill and Penelope Bonnett, *Nature in the Urban Landscape: A Study of City Ecosystems* (Baltimore, 1973).

David E. Davis, "The Role of Intraspecific Competition in Game Management," *Transactions of the Fourteenth North American Wildlife and Natural Resources Conference, March 7-9, 1949* (Washington, 1949), pp. 225-231.

William B. Jackson, "Food Habits of Baltimore, Maryland, Cats in Relation to Rat Populations," *Journal of Mammalogy*, 32 (1951), pp. 458-461.

D. Summers-Smith, *The House Sparrow* (London, 1963).

Charles F. Walcutt, "Changes in Bird Life in Cambridge, Massachusetts from 1860 to 1964," *Auk*, 91 (January, 1974), pp. 151-160.

Aelred D. Geis, "The New Town Bird Quadrille," *Natural History*, 83 (June-July, 1974), pp. 56-60.

Terry Gumpertz, "Some Observations on the Feral Pigeon in London," *Bird Study*, 4 (1957), pp. 2-13.

CHAPTER VI.

Massachusetts Department of Environmental Quality Engineering, "History of Air Pollution Regulation in Massachusetts" (mimeograph, no date).

Reid A. Bryson and John E. Kutzbach, *Air Pollution*, Association of American Geographers, Committee on College Geography, Resource Paper No. 2 (Washington, 1968).

Amasa B. Ford, *Urban Public Health* (New York, 1976).

Massachusetts Department of Environmental Quality Engineering, "Monthly Monitoring Reports" (Xerox, Boston, 1976).

Metropolitan Area Planning Council, *Metropolitan Boston Bikeways* (Boston, February, 1976).

Barry Commoner, *The Poverty of Power* (New York, 1976), pp. 176-177.

Massachusetts Division of Water Resources, Water Resources Commission, *Groundwater and Groundwater Law in Massachusetts* (Boston, 1976).

Ernest M. Gould, Jr., "Values, Trees, and The Urban Realm," Symposium on Trees and Forests in an Urbanizing Environment, University of Massachusetts, August 18-21, 1970, Holdsworth Natural Resources Center, Planning and Resource Development Series, No. 17 (Amherst, Mass., 1971), pp. 79-90.

Hydrologic Engineering Section, Water Control Branch, New England Division, U. S. Army Corps of Engineers, "Effects of Urbanization on Peak Runoff" (mimeograph, Waltham, Mass., June, 1973).

R. A. Brackley, W. R. Fleck, and W. R. Meyer, *Hydrology and Water Resources of the Neponset and Weymouth River Basins, Massachusetts,* United States Geological Survey, Atlas HA-484 (Washington, 1973).

Michael H. Frimpter, "Preliminary Single-Purpose Report, Ground-Water Hydrology, South Eastern New England," United States Geological Survey, Open File Report (Boston, January, 1973).

Kennedy Engineers, Inc., *National Science Foundation Phase One Engineering Report: Boston Case Study* (San Francisco, 1976).

Massachusetts Executive Office of Environmental Affairs, *Massachusetts Water Supply Policy Study* (Boston, January, 1977).

Joel A. Tarr and Francis Clay McMichael, "Decisions About Wastewater Technology, 1850-1932," *Journal of the Water Resources Planning Management Division, ASCE,* 103 (May, 1977), pp. 47-61.

Fred Basselman and David Callies, *The Quiet Revolution in Land,* United States Executive Office of the President, Council on Environmental Quality (Washington, 1972).

Seymour I. Toll, *The Zoned American* (New York, 1969).

Massachusetts Department of Community Affairs, Bureau of Regional Planning, *Enabling Legislation for Planning and Zoning,* Study Report No. 2, *Municipal Planning and Subdivision* (Boston, February, 1973).

Rhode Island Development Council, Planning Division, *Land Use Controls in Rhode Island,* Publication No. 6 (Providence, March 1963).

Massachusetts Association of Conservation Commissions, *Massachusetts Conservation Commission Handbook,* Robert J. Ellis, ed. (Boston, 1973).

CHAPTER VII.

David Halberstam, "CBS: The Power and the Profits," 2 parts, *Atlantic Monthly* (January, February, 1976), pp. 33-71, 52-91.

John Tebbel, *The Media in America* (New York, 1974).

E. M. Forster, "The Machine Stops," *Collected Tales of E. M. Forster* (New York, 1971), pp. 144-197.

Edward Bellamy, *Looking Backward: 2000-1887* (Boston, 1888).

Ebenezer Howard, *Garden Cities of To-morrow* (1898, reprinted Cambridge, 1965).

Lewis Mumford, *The Pentagon of Power* (New York, 1970).

John Updike, *Couples* (New York, 1968).

Marius Bewley, "Scott Fitzgerald's Criticism of America," *Sewanee Review,* 62 (Spring, 1954), pp. 223-246.

F. Scott Fitzgerald, *The Great Gatsby* (New York, 1925, reprinted ca. 1953).

CHAPTER VIII.

Herbert I. Schiller, *The Mind Managers* (Boston, 1973).

Allan Dundes and Carl R. Pagter, *Urban Folklore from the Paperwork Empire* (Austin, Texas, 1975). Reproduced by permission of the American Folklore Society from URBAN FOLKLORE FROM THE PAPERWORK EMPIRE, American Folklore Society Memoir Series, Vol. 62: 78, 1975. NOT FOR FURTHER REPRODUCTION.

Michael Young and Peter Willmott, *The Symmetrical Family* (New York, 1973), Chapter 10.

Robert Scholes, *Structural Fabulation* (Notre Dame, Indiana, 1975).

Saul Bellow, *Mr. Sammler's Planet* (New York, 1969).

Olive Higgins Prouty, *Pencil Shavings* (Boston, 1961).

———, *Stella Dallas* (Boston, 1923).

Theodore Sturgeon, "Slow Sculpture," in *Sturgeon Is Alive and Well* (New York, 1971), pp. 88-89.